DiRTY STOP OUTS GUIDE TO 1970s COVENTRY

A quiet night with the Specials
Photo: James Melik

More pictures/ more memories/ more excuses to feel 18 again

Ruth Cherrington asserts the moral right to be identified as the authors of this work.
A catalogue record for this book is available from the British Library.

Published by Dirty Stop Outs Ltd.

Other titles in this series:

Dirty Stop Out's Guide to 1970s Manchester.

Dirty Stop Out's Guide to 1970s Liverpool.

Dirty Stop Out's Guide to 1970s Coventry.

Dirty Stop Out's Guide to 1970s Barnsley.

Dirty Stop Out's Guide to 1950s Sheffield.

Dirty Stop Out's Guide to 1960s Sheffield.

Dirty Stop Out's Guide to 1970s Sheffield.

Dirty Stop Out's Guide to 1980s Sheffield.

Dirty Stop Out's Guide to 1980s Sheffield – King Mojo Edition

Dirty Stop Out's Guide to 1990s Sheffield.

Dirty Stop Out's Guide to 1970s Chesterfield.

Dirty Stop Out's Guide to 1970s Sheffield – Club Fiesta Edition.

Dirty Stop Out's Guide to 1980s Chesterfield.

Dirty Stop Out's Guide to 1980s Coventry.

Dirty Stop Outs Guide to Working Men's Clubs.

Dirty Stop Out's Guide to Coventry's Working Men's Clubs

Dirty Stop Out's Guide to 1980s Sheffield – The Limit Edition

Dirty Stop Out's Guide to 1980s Chesterfield Quizbook.

Dirty Stop Out's Guide to 1990s Chesterfield.

Dirty Stop Out's Guide to 1980s Sheffield – Wapentake Edition.

Dirty Stop Outs Guide to 1980s Chesterfield – In Pictures.

Dirty Stop Outs Guide to Sheffield – Rebels Edition.

We're on the look out for writers to cover other UK towns and cities and we're always on the look out for great retro photos! Please email us at **info@dirtystopouts.com** if you fancy getting involved.

DiRTY STOP OUTS GUIDE TO 1970s COVENTRY

Miranda Aston and friends at a gig on Hearsall Common

More pictures/ more memories/ more excuses to feel 18 again

Coventry icon Pauline Black performing in the late '70s (above and front cover) Photo: Pete Hill

CONTENTS

DiRTY STOP OUTS GUIDE

The Specials in action Photos - James Melik

A special edition for a special decade – revisiting 1970s Coventry

FOREWORD

Below: Khayyam at the Climax pub Photo - Chis N. Jones

Welcome to this special edition of the 'Dirty Stop Outs Guide to 1970s Coventry'!
It's hard to believe that six years have passed since the original book hit the bookshops. Packed with memories, stories, pics, and memorabilia of Coventry's nighttime and daytime leisure activities, it quickly became a must-buy read.

It proved very popular amongst '70s pub crawlers, live music lovers, disco dancers, café bar and take-away regulars. Those who played in bands or were DJs featured in the book and became big fans.

It struck a chord with Dirty Stop Outs near and far, with copies being read as far away as the USA, Thailand, Canada, and Australia!

No one worried about being sent to Coventry in the 1970s: people made the most of all that was on offer. Many are still doing just that, even if there are a few creaking joints on the dancefloor now!

Work often got in the way, but how else were you going to pay for those new platform shoes or loons? Let alone the beers, gigs, and records.

The popularity of the 1970s book brought motivation to write the 1980s Dirty Stop Outs Guide, which came out the following year. Coventry's wide network of Working Men's Clubs was second to none and earned its own chapter in the original 1970s book. But with so much going on in over 60 clubs, they deserved a Dirty Stop Outs Guide to themselves. And they got just that in 2020.

During the past six years, Coventry's City of Culture Year has come and gone. Delayed due to circumstances beyond our control, it was nevertheless enthusiastically celebrated and enjoyed by many. The long wait and patience were rewarded with many events and activities going on right across Coventry.

Part of this was an eye-catching mural outside Pool

Carrie and the mural team

Midnight Circus, playing at the Memorial Park
Photo - Nigel Clemons

Artist Carrie Reichardt working on the mural Photo - Carrie Reichardt

Meadow bus station, which award-winning artist Carrie Reichardt was specially commissioned to design.
This is a wonderful, tiled tribute not only to Coventry's renowned music scene, including 2-Tone but also to its people.

And we're very proud to see so many of our Dirty Stop Out visuals prominently featured in this mural!

There are familiar faces and places here!

2022 saw celebrations of the 50th anniversary of Coventry band Lieutenant Pigeon's 'Mouldy Old Dough' reaching the No.1 spot. An unlikely hit but hard to forget even if you want to!

There were further celebrations in 2022 as Pauline Black of The Selecter was appointed Officer of the Order of the British Empire (OBE) for services to entertainment. Another well-deserved award for Pauline was being appointed as a Deputy Lieutenant of the West Midlands in May of the same year. Congratulations to Pauline for all she's done for Coventry and music.

And 2023 brought the 50th Anniversary of the Coventry Hobo, which helped to promote all things musical and remains a brilliant archive.

Sadly, we've lost some Dirty Stop Outs and great musicians, with Terry Hall among them. We remember them here.

We were asked to do an updated 1970s book so many times that it seemed rude not to. After much thought and

a few false starts, the time came to write this special edition. More people offered their memories and pics, including DJs, drummers, dancers, and darts players.

We've packed in as much as possible, keeping most of the existing content but with some new, never-seen-before material.

This includes a lot more about local bands and the 'circuit,' which spread into every nook and cranny across the city. The number of bands popping up was described by local music fan and writer Pete Clemons as 'euphoric, incredibly exhilarating'. Many had large fan bases, and some found fame. Miranda Aston believes that "Coventry was one of the leading places for punk. It was like manna from heaven for us!"

There are stories about those who became DJs almost by accident, with some of them still spinning discs across the globe.

You'll even find here some '70s inspired poetry from a few local bards!

We also say a big 'thank you' to two of Coventry's great movers and shakers from the '70s who continue to promote Coventry's musical and cultural heritage to this day: Pete Chambers and Trev Teasdel.

We hope you enjoy revisiting 1970s Coventry, reading about the great places where people found fun, friends, and lifelong attachments!

INTRODUCTION

Look up, look down – loads of places to stop out all around

Ruins of the old Cathedral become a site of reconciliation

There was still very much that looked brand spanking new, mixing well with the old and quaint in 1970s Coventry. And we're not just talking about the residents.

After heavy bombing during World War Two, much of the city centre had been reduced to rubble. The sight of the smouldering remains of centuries-old St. Michael's Cathedral the morning after the blitz of November 14th,

> **"When I think back to the old days of the 70s, I know how lucky I was to have been around during those great times."**
> Colin Horton

1940, became an iconic image of Coventry's suffering.

But by the early 1970s, with the new Cathedral designed by Sir Basil Spence standing proudly alongside the ruins, there was a sense of optimism about the future. The remains of the old Cathedral had become a site of reconciliation and cultural exchange, with the International Centre located there.

Like the fabled phoenix, Coventry re-emerged from the ashes: a modern city that inspired civic pride. 'Made in Coventry' was an expression not just reserved for cars!

There was a pleasant traffic-free Precinct shopping area, with murals, fountains, benches, cherry trees, and flowers. Coventry people enjoyed looking around the shops and market, perhaps having a cuppa or a bite to eat. Many popular nightspots were also there within walking distance of each other.

We were spoilt for choice in terms of where to dance, eat, or just hang out with pubs, clubs, and cafés galore right across the city. Colleges such as the Lanchester Polytechnic (now Coventry University) joined in the fun, providing yet more leisure options in their expanding Student Union facilities.

Those with enough energy and money in their pockets could go out every night of the week, each time to somewhere different. It would surprise folk now just how many did go out every night, even if it meant sneaking out of work when on night shift!

Increasing numbers of residents lived on new, out-of-town estates with decent housing and plenty of green spaces. They would travel into town on brown and cream Corporation buses, seeking friendly faces and fun after a hard day's graft in one of the many factories,

> Trev Teasdel: **"I grew up with a brand new city centre and a brand new estate with lots of grass and trees, a different scenario from the old back to backs. It gave me a sense of optimism."**

The new Cathedral
designed by Sir
Basil Spence

Lady Godiva in Broadgate with Hotel Leofric and Owen Owen in background

shops, and offices. Coventry was also a magnet for those living in nearby Rugby and Nuneaton.

1970s Coventry was very much an industrial city, built by generations of working people coming from across the UK and beyond to make a living and a home. Cars were king and anything relating to their production with Standard Triumph, Jaguar, and Chrysler all in the city.

Machine tools manufacturer Alfred Herberts was a major employer, as were the long-established Courtaulds. Alvis, GEC, and tractor giants Massey Ferguson were also in town. There was coal mining as well with pretty much full employment at the start of the decade.

Sue Long: **"Such good memories of my teenage years in the early 70s. I could probably bore for Britain with all the bands I saw in Coventry around that time. Wasn't it great!"**

Later in the 70s, industrial decline set in, and the city's leisure sector was hit hard as unemployment took its toll. Dirty Stop Outs kept calm and carried on going out, not letting things like power cuts, three-day working weeks, and lighter pay packets keep them at home too much.

Most workers received actual pay packets back then - small brown envelopes with their money and pay slip inside, usually handed out on Thursdays. The weekend started then and for many lasted until the money ran out. Before February 1971, we had pounds, shillings (bobs), and pence, but then decimalization changed all that. We got a bit mixed up to begin with and things seemed dearer, but we got used to it.

"The 70s came, and things I had thought of in passing were now coming to the fore, things like girls and music, and being part of something, hell I don't know what, just something!"
Teenaged local music fan and writer Pete Chambers

Ray King, Coventry's first black singer, and international star, summed it up nicely: "All we were really into was having fun over the weekend. We worked hard through the week."

There was also talk about whether to join the Common Market or not. Labour Leader Harold Wilson advised 'stay out' in 1971, but in 1973 Prime Minister Edward Heath took us in anyway.

Many left school at 15, started work right away, and soon got into the habit of going out, if they hadn't already! Pubs were far more than 'drinking dens' as we shall see, offering all kinds of entertainment, which is why many of them are remembered so fondly throughout this book.

Built in Coventry
for the highways of the world.
Jaguar Daimler Triumph

Workers at the Rootes plant, Humber Lane

Triumph Toledo economy at Henlys
HENLYS

View of the shopping precinct

Coventry's Precinct

Look up! Meet me under the elephant

Where would a 'typical' night out start? Often in a pub but local landmarks were good places to wait for mates before heading off together. Meeting under the elephant high on a pole in Broadgate was popular. The elephant with a castle on its back is Coventry's coat of arms. Later in the decade the new sports centre alongside the Olympic swimming pool was built elephant shaped.

> Paul Sadler: **"The nightlife in the '70s was like something you would not see today! You could let your hair down and just enjoy yourself."**

For Nick Edgington, it was "under the horse's tail" - meaning the statue of Lady Godiva on her horse. The legend of this famous lady plays a large role in Coventry's heritage. She is said to have ridden naked through the streets of the medieval city with only her long tresses covering her modesty. Married to the Earl of Leofric, she was protesting against his plan to raise taxes on the poor citizens.

Precinct mural and the fountain minus the water!

Linda Kendall and friend Kim at Lady Godiva statue

Linda Kendall and friend Susan at Lady Godiva statue

The story goes that he abandoned his plans after his wife's naked ride and Lady Godiva became an important symbol of the city. Perhaps we can call Lady Godiva an original 'rude girl'?

Linda Kendall and her friends gathered at the Godiva statue one memorable evening in June 1976 when they were celebrating their 18th birthdays and finishing 'A' levels. "We met there before going down to the Locarno ready to meet our guests."

Miranda Aston: **"Late '70s night out for me - start with tuna sandwich at the Wedge followed by the Dive, the Rose and Crown, back red room at the Bear, Mr George's, Tiffany's, La Chaumiere in the Burges and finish with fish 'n' chips from Parson's Nose. Now all gone, but wow, what a night! And so glad they were there when I was a teenager."**

Hotel Leofric - popular meeting place

Richard Hil (centre) and mates outside the Greyhound Pub

Lady Godiva has been moved a few times over the years but now stands in Broadgate again.

Mark Rewhorn and Sue Lowe both favoured the main entrance to the Owen and Owen department store as a meeting point. This modern five storey building overlooking Broadgate was another place to look up to and embodied Coventry's revival. Often referred to as the 'top of the town', Broadgate was the place to head for on New Year's Eve, being Coventry's own version of Trafalgar Square.

Next to Owens was the luxurious Leofric Hotel, a handy meet up point as well as a place for refreshments. Opened in 1955, it was another of Coventry's iconic buildings, with a ballroom, banqueting and conference facilities. It was also one of the first new hotels built in Britain after the war and was a symbol not only of Coventry's recovery but of the whole country's.

Many actors performing at Coventry Theatre and other celebrities passed through its doors. It was quite classy. Not so classy were the Sex Pistols who caused an

Sex Pistols following the trashing of a Leofric

outrage when they stayed there after their gig at Mr George's nightclub in December 1977. Sid Vicious, in traditional rock 'n' roll style, smashed up his room.

Many nights out were rounded off with a takeaway and the Parson's Nose was one of the most popular. Coventry 2-Tone band The Specials were known to pop in for a 'one-all-in' of faggots, peas and chips now and then.

Whether meeting up at the Locarno, under the Elephant or any of the wide range of venues, Coventry Dirty Stop Outs had plenty of choice.

We shed light on and celebrate those memories of the city's vast array night and day activities, the bands, discos, fashions and films.

Right: Wild Boys hit the press
Photo: Rob Lapworth

September 18. 1979

page seven

Hardcore from the Wild Boys

THE Wild Boys are a four-piece Coventry punk outfit who have been playing with their present line-up since December last year.

Between them, however, they have quite a range of musical backgrounds and for most of them, the Wild Boys is not their first excursion into the music scene.

The members of the band are Johnnie T on lead vocals and rhythm guitar, Marc Extra on lead guitar and backing vocals, Rob Lapworth on bass and Fly Lynch on drums.

It was Johnnie and Marc who got together first. They knew each other from Keresley Village and had both been to Keresley Newlands School (though they were not in the same year.

Homicide

Together they were in a group called Demented, quite a basic band who didn't do very much apart from a few youth club gigs. Rob was introduced by a friend and, with Demented disbanded, the Extras were born.

● Drummer Fly.

drums last December they have done quite a few gigs, namely the Heath, Swanswell, Lanchester Poly and the Zodiac plus the Fighting Cocks in Birmingham and the Crown in Leamington Spa.

Their gig at the Heath with Clique and Homicide they rate as their best so far.

Three of the Boys have full time jobs, and for Rob and Marc the Careers Centre has been instrumental (!) in finding them work.

Johnnie got his job as a control room operator through his own efforts while Marc applied for and was successful in getting a job as a trainee butcher through an advertisement in Jobhunter.

Rob, who went to Finham Park School, is now an apprentice draughtsman, but when he left school he was informed by the

Jobhunter Group of the Month

The Extras played a softer brand of music than the lads play today, and, with the discovery that there was a London group of the same name, the boys changed their name and image to what we know today, hardcore punk.

At their first gig as the Wild Boys they played as a trio — that was at the Golden Eagle in Keresley.

Careers Centre of a vacancy for a photographer with ICA Studios.

Rob says he found the Careers Centre very helpful and says that his apprenticeship comes first.

Specials

When they started playing, the Wild Boys had to pay their own expenses. One of them sold a motorbike to get their equipment.

Any money they earn goes back into the band. So far they haven't

had any financial worries because they have full-time jobs.

Their only problem has been a place to practise — at present they have nowhere to rehearse but in Johnnie's mum's front room.

As far as musical backgrounds are concerned, Fly has been playing drums since the tender age of seven. His father was a professional drummer for a number of years and has passed his experience on to Fly.

Marc would also like to have learned drums but his family could not afford to buy him a kit, so guitar, was his second choice.

Marc's brother is Roddy Radiation of the Specials and Marc would like to emphasise that Roddy did not teach him to play guitar, although of course, he acknowledges that Roddy has been very influential in his development.

So what would the group like to be their next step?

Well apart from to keep playing live gigs and enjoy themselves, they would like to put out a flexi disc if they can raise the money. Their choice of number would be We're Only Monsters — the song that is most popular with the crowd and which I would definitely their best song.

● Three of the Wild Boys, Johnnie, Marc and Rob. Rob's the one whose movements were a bit too quick for the camera shutter.

Coventry's Oldest Pub- The Golden Cross

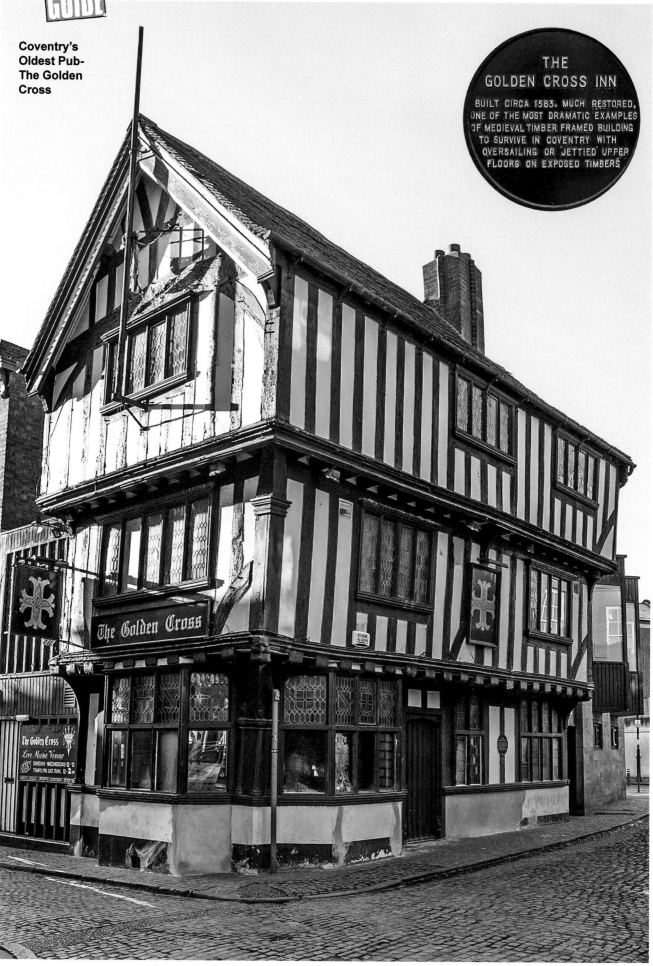

THE GOLDEN CROSS INN

BUILT CIRCA 1583. MUCH RESTORED, ONE OF THE MOST DRAMATIC EXAMPLES OF MEDIEVAL TIMBER FRAMED BUILDING TO SURVIVE IN COVENTRY WITH OVERSAILING OR 'JETTIED' UPPER FLOORS ON EXPOSED TIMBERS

THE NIGHT STARTS AT A PUB BUT WHICH ONE?

Many great nights out began with a good old-fashioned pub crawl. Coventry was well served with pubs, with the older ones that had avoided bomb damage, those that had been rebuilt, and some lovely new ones added to the mix.

It wasn't just about drinking. A pub crawl was a great way to see who was out and about and got people into the mood for the night ahead. Old mates met up, and new ones were made - social networking long before the term was invented! There was also the chance of romance, whether a brief encounter or something more long-lasting.

Most pubs offered some sort of music: live bands, DJs, discos, a jukebox. You could even listen to poetry in some or just have a quiet pint!

Friends gathered in their preferred pubs before heading to one of the city's nightclubs. They might have just one drink in each as 'time' was called at 10.30 back then. Woe betide the pub manager who allowed extra time.

'Lock-ins' did happen in some pubs for those in the know, including CID and other police officers. Lizzi Maxted learned how to spot them when she was a barmaid at the Albany pub. "They used to come in for a late drink most nights. The leather jackets and shoulder-length hair were always a giveaway!"

But which pub first? For Colin Horton and mates, Friday and Saturday nights always started at the Alhambra. "We would then move to the Silver Sword, the Penny Black, Three Tuns, Climax, Thistle and Market Tavern, the Mercia". The Alhambra and Silver Sword (aka the Dirty Dagger!) were literally just a short stagger from each other. Eventually, even miraculously, they made it to the Locarno!

Stuart Beamish, left, with friends

Stuart Beamish: **"The gaffer when I first drank at the Golden Cross was Cyril and his wife Olive, later it was Mick and Jayne, then it was a guy with Brutus, a huge Rottweiler."**

Saturday nights for Tony Unwin and his mates usually started off at Coventry's oldest pub, the Golden Cross. It had survived the Blitz even though the nearby old Cathedral hadn't.

Dating back to 1583, the 'Cross' has had many ghostly sightings. This didn't deter committed regulars nor musicians, though some DJs complained of 'unexplained' electrical problems.

Gill Dawson:**"Going to the pubs was about the music, the atmosphere, and being out with friends, having a good time, not about getting drunk."**

Gill Dawson didn't see any ghosts, but she thought the 'older' crowd, denim and leather-clad bikers, were pretty frightening! "I was an early feminist, and I saw some biker girls wearing badges saying, 'This is property of so and so,' their boyfriends, of course. I was shocked! I wanted to tell them they weren't the property of any man, but I didn't dare do so."

Stuart Beamish reckons there was an invisible dividing line down the pub. "People either drank one end or the other. Some would have said it was rough, with denim and leather as the dress code, but it was a friendly pub. You could always get a game of darts, and fights were rare. The jukebox was loud and had a great selection of music. Cider was the preferred drink among the regulars."

Richard Hil and friends at the Greyhound

Richard Hil: **"The Greyhound pub was great! All peeling paint, wooden floors, low ceilings, and glorious hand-pumped beer. We sat in one of the small rooms pontificating on this and that, mainly football and politics, and perhaps young women."**

Stuart was there the night of November 1974 when the IRA tried to bomb the telephone exchange. "We felt it, rather than heard it, as the music was so loud!"

Tucked away in Much Park Street, near the 'cop shop,' was the Greyhound, which dated back to the 18th century. In the early '70s, it looked like it had seen better days, but it was a very popular pub with a lot going on. Richard Hil and his schoolmates were among its many customers, and he was very fond of the beer. "It served Marston's Pedigree ale - my favorite beer, ever!"

Others enjoyed the darts matches. Stuart Beamish played darts there "when Craig Shakespeare was the gaffer."

Opposite the Coventry Theatre was the mock Tudor-style Smithfield Hotel, built in the 19th century. It was named after London's Smithfield market as it was on the site of the old cattle market. Apart from attracting the theatre crowd, it also had live music, including the band White Rum, who regularly played at the Locarno. John Starkey saw his first stripper at the Smithfield.

Another mock Tudor pub was the Tally Ho, on the corner of the Burges. Refurbished in the late 1960s, it had a restaurant with waitresses wearing neat red waistcoats, a nod to the hunting theme. The smoky, low-ceilinged cellar bar, with very loud music, was the perfect spot for young people.

The names of some newer pubs reflected Coventry's great industrial heritage. The Climax was named after the manufacturers of Cooper Climax and Lotus F-1

car engines. Opened in 1962 in the City Arcade, near the birdcage, it was often packed. Gill Dawson and friends went there and says it was popular with younger people.

Gill recalls a night when the DJ warned those under 18 to leave quickly because of an imminent police raid. They soon returned when it was over. Underage drinking is not to be condoned, but teenagers were out for fun with friends, and often one drink lasted the whole night. Many would already have been in full-time work and earning a living, having left school at 15 or 16 after 1972.

The Herald in Canley was named after the popular car produced in the nearby Standard Triumph factory. It was very handy for workers as they piled out on Thursday evenings clutching their pay packets before the wives got hold of them! The Herald also got a lot of custom from staff at the 'Cov Rad' (Coventry Radiator and Presswork Company), which was just across the street. The plant, the largest manufacturers of radiators in the country, had been in Canley since 1960.

The 'Jag' (Jaguar) on Corporation Street was named after the famous cars produced in the city. Car manufacturing employed many thousands in the 1970s, either on the 'track' - assembly line - or other parts of the production process and related industries. But on a night out, work was the last thing on people's minds!

The Market Tavern stood right next to the City's now-listed circular market. Meryl Barrett had her first drink there. "Vodka and lime. I was just 14!" Robin Moorcroft remembers it being popular with 'first-time around mods who congregated there before going dancing at the Locarno. Their suits, short haircuts, and lashings of aftershave were still the norm.'

Herald Lodge on the site of former Herald pub

Sue Lowe favored the Bear in the High Street. "It was a rock pub, with guys wearing a lot of denim, leather, or velvet jackets, T-shirts with various band names emblazoned across the front, and longish hair."

Her parents thought she was being a bit rebellious going there but says "it wasn't really hardcore." It was about the music, dancing, and meeting nice young men! She once downed a pint of Newcastle Brown Ale faster than any of the other girls there and won a copy of The Who 'Live at Leeds' LP, which she still has.

> Sue Lowe: **"Cocktails at Ray's Bar were just part of Coventry in the 1970s. Ray always seemed like such a nice man!"**

Local drummer John Hewitt was a Bear regular. "A great atmosphere, never any trouble. Good beer too. It was where you could find musicians from many local bands - Gods Toys, Urge, Wild Boys, and more. I knew everyone in those days."

The Herald, Canley

Sue Lowe and friends would call in at the Rocket, near the train station, for a swift half and a "hello" to her boyfriend, a part-time barman there in 1973-4. Nick Edgington started drinking at the Rocket when still a pupil at nearby King Henry VIII School. "Most lads did, but too many teachers went there."

The Rocket was the nearest 'watering hole' to the Horizon recording studios. Local music historian Pete Chambers remembers bands going there for breaks and refreshment during long recording sessions. "They often sat there talking about different musical ideas and things they were going to do when they got back in the studio."

> Ray Barrie: **"Just like most bands who have recorded at Horizon, when the evening session was completed, we all ran over to the Rocket pub for a few late beers."**

Another 'rock pub' was the Godiva ('Dive Bar'), where Robin Moorcroft hung out with friends. "We thought we were part of some developing revolution whilst drinking copious amounts of IPA or, even worse, Watney's Red Barrel, smoking Embassy or No 6. The Dive had that brilliant, listed collage wrapped around the wall that gave it the air of some hip gallery."

It was popular with students from the nearby 'Lanch' Poly. The music included the underground

Precinct with Market Tavern in background

Market Tavern

The Lady Godiva

sounds from the States, such as Bob Dylan, Jimi Hendrix, says Robin. "Any band that was given the cool description of being called 'underground,' even if they did appear on 'Top of the Pops'."

John D'Arcy liked to kick off the night with a cocktail at Ray's Bar in the Leofric Hotel. "Black Russian for me, please!" Sue Lowe's cocktail of choice there was Brandy Alexander, but Ray Rastall could concoct many delectable mixes. He had been serving drinks at the Leofric since it first opened in 1955, and his dedication was recognized with the hotel naming the bar after him. Ray was quite a local legend!

The Leofric also had a more traditional pub, the White Lion, for those preferring something less fussy.

For a bit of sing-along, oompah-oompah style, the Bier Kellar was the place to be. There were the large glasses

The Albany

and general revelry. Why go all the way to Munich? It morphed into the Dog and Trumpet in 1977 and soon became a favorite music venue as well as a watering hole.

There were a few sing-alongs going over at the Cottage in Earlsdon, not far from the city centre, which was much loved by Val Haudiquet.

> Nick Edgington: **"The Specials headquarters were across the road at no. 51, so they were regulars at the Albany."**

"The regulars sang all the old favorites. One magical evening a lady walked in wearing a dress Shirley Bassey would have been happy to own, all tight with a frill around the bottom. She got up to sing, a hush of expectation settled round the room. We all recognized the opening lines... 'Look at me I'm off to sunny Spain,'

and then came the immortal 'Yes me and my spaniel.'"

Valerie wishes she could have bottled the atmosphere that night!

Stuart Beamish also enjoyed these nights. "Wal and Sheila kept a great pub. Wal would call up his favorites to sing songs like 'Delilah' and 'Danny Boy.' Jerry Dammers playing boogie-woogie on the piano some lunchtimes.

The Albany in Earlsdon had opened in the early 20th century. Nick Edgington and mates started using it around 1977 after abandoning the Rocket. "Great pub for music, cheap beer, and pool tables upstairs. We were in the pool room most weekends."

> Tony Unwin: **"We used to go to the Bear, which had some unpleasant bouncers manning the disco. A couple in the Penny Black, then finally the Three Tuns, by which time it was about half ten. It fair brings a tear to my eye recounting these happy days!"**

Coventry Cross, the Burges

Tales from behind the Bar!

Lizzi Maxted had her first 'proper' job as a barmaid in 1977.

"I had just left Barr's Hill Grammar for Girls school, and I got a holiday job in Bob's Grocery shop across from the Albany. That was when I first met Anne, who offered me a full-time job at her pub. I told her that I was only 16, but she was not deterred and told me to tell anyone who asked that I was a glass collector!"

While working there, Lizzi learned how they made the mild. 'Seriously, you don't want to know!' She memorized the price of drinks, which were the most popular with the ladies, and also what a kidney wiper was! She also saw the perils of over-drinking. It didn't seem a problem that she was only 16, something we hear about quite often.

Lizzi remembers the other barmaids. "Alice, with her lovely beehive to make her look taller (she was tiny), and Scottish Jess. They taught me a lot. Sylvia was a few years older than me, it seemed like a lot back then, and she was dating Brad, the drummer from a band that used to rehearse across Broomfield Road at a garage."

Which band was that then? Lizzi was talking about the Specials before they were famous. With the Albany being their local plus gigging there, it earned the label of the 'home' of 2-Tone music.

Lizzi couldn't know back then what a historic time it was, nor that she'd be working there at another one decades later. In 2017, she was the landlady on a short-term lease. When this ended, time was called, and after 110 years, the Albany closed.

Miranda Aston liked the Albany because it was one pub where she and other punks could get served! Many pub managers saw punks as threatening in the early days around 1976/77 as there was much damning coverage about the scene in the media. They often threw punks out... sometimes literally. It was a relatively short period, Miranda tells us, but very unpleasant.

Valerie Haudiquet lived just across the street from the Albany. "We would have some good drinking sessions there. Sunday lunchtime sessions were much more sedate. Drinking game time. Who knew the answer to questions about the Archers, that type of thing!"

Val worked one summer behind the bar of another local pub, the Royal Oak, which was "slightly more refined." She has fond memories of serving drinks to a Swedish football team one Sunday.

The Foleshill area had some old pubs, and the General Wolfe stands out. There were many great gigs in this old Victorian drinking establishment with local bands playing alongside more well-known ones.

When Sue Lowe did day release at Tile Hill College in 1975-6, she visited the nearby Newlands pub with her friend beforehand. "Trying to learn shorthand was virtually impossible after drinking two or three sweet martini and lemonades (yuk!), or, in my friend's case, vodka and lime."

The many pubs right across the city offered different atmospheres, music genres, food, and fashions. And there were some where you could play darts, cards, or just have a quiet drink.

General Wolfe, Foleshill

Punks at General Wolfe
Photo: Rob Lapworth

DiRTY STOP OUTS GUiDE

APOLLO THEATRE, Coventry

Derek Block in assoc. with Dave Woods presents

Siouxsie and The Banshees

Saturday, 29th August 1981
Evening 7-30

STALLS
£3.50

V   34

No Ticket exchanged nor money refunded.
No Cameras or Recording Equipment.
Official Programmes sold only in the Theatre.

A. B. Cooper (Printers) Ltd. MANCHESTER

Retain this portion

NTS
ENDERS
1197
UARY
NTRY
£1.50

TIFFANY'S (Thurs) OCTOBER 11th *1979*

GAMBINNI PROMOTIONS PROUDLY PRESENT

THE INCREDIBLE

Angelic Upstarts

+ GUESTS

SQUAD + RIOT ACT

DISCO TILL 2 am LATE BARS

Tickets £2.00 in advance

TIFFANYS
Box Office open 10-5 weekdays
8.00 p.m. (Normal Sessions)
Telephone: Coventry 24570

**THURSDAY
MAY 79   10**

at 7.30 p.m. (Bar)

Straight Music presents

IGGY POP

No   700

This portion to be retained
(P.T.O.)

TIFFANY'S
Box Office open 10-5 weekdays
8pm (Normal Sessions)
Telephone: Coventry 24570

**THURSDAY
FEBRUARY   7**
1980
at 8.00 p.m. (BAR)

STRAIGHT MUSIC presents

THE CLASH

No   805

This portion to be retained
(P.T.O.)

FINAL SOLUTION

BACKSTAGE PASS

ARTIST SLITS 79
VENUE COVENTRY
SIGNED

Punk gig tickets from Miranda Aston's collection

CHAPTER 2

THE LOCARNO AND A STAIRWAY TO HEAVEN

Stairway to heaven!

Without a doubt one of Coventry's favourite places to dance the night away was the Locarno Ballroom. Opened in August 1960, it was sleek, modern and dominated the skyline of Coventry's Precinct. Mecca Leisure gave locals something to look up to, literally.

There was ballroom dancing in its early years. It will always be remembered for its revolving stage, glitter balls, balconies overlooking the dancefloor, the Long Bar and Bali Hai Suite. It hosted and boasted a wide variety of entertainment including DJs.

It very quickly became the place to be. Many referred to as the 'Rockhouse,' because, well, it rocked! Just about every well-known band appeared there at some point as well as many local ones.

Annette Williscroft: **"Friday night was Locarno night for us. We went to the Market Tavern or some other pub to start. No good going before 10 pm as it hadn't got started."**

The fun started young with the popular Saturday morning 'nightclub training' for Coventry's teenagers at the 'ever-so good' Locarno. The matinee discos became an institution and the young 'uns queued up with nervous excitement. Once they'd earned their stripes they could move on to the evening and the well-into-the-night sessions.

It was a sort of Dirty Stop Out coming of age.

Meryl Barrett: **"Aged about 15 we "graduated" from the matinee slots to Monday nights, getting the last bus home. I remember local DJ Pete Waterman playing lots of soul and reggae and some rather rude tracks for us as young teens such as 'Wet Dream' and ones by Judge Dredd."**

DJ Pete used the under-18s matinees to gauge what got the kids on the dancefloor and what emptied it and how their tastes differed from those a few years older.

Meryl Barrett remembers there used to be bands on Saturday mornings and she saw Mungo Jerry. "I missed Bay City Rollers as my friend didn't tell me she was going- I was so cross!"

BBC Radio 1 DJ Noel Edmonds was one of many guest DJs who spun the discs. There was also the 'Dancing DJ Danny'.

Young Locarno fan Meryll Barrett

Above:
Bali Hai Disco ticket
Left: Linda Kendall celebrating with friends, Bali Hai Suite, 1976

Robin Moorcroft describes the Bali Hai suite as "a classic 70s club room with a South Seas theme like the Castaways in Birmingham". He hired it many times for parties and recalls the Bali Hai's plastic palms. "There was even more plastic with large mirror balls and fake red leather seating."

Meryl Barrett tried to get in one night but was turned away for being too young. She managed it on another occasion and kept a plastic leaf from there as a souvenir!

In June 1976, Linda Kendall and a group of friends booked the Bali Hai to celebrate their 18th birthdays. "I remember it was free to book on a Monday. The club had some ultraviolet lights so if you were wearing a white bra it would show through your clothes!"

> Colin Horton: **"I would sometimes 'sneak into the bogs for a crafty fag on Saturday mornings at the Locarno. You got thrown out if bouncers caught you. I did many times!"**

Linda can't remember the party too well, apart from being bought lots of drinks. "When the lights went on at the end of the night, I was in a clinch with someone very nice - although probably anyone would've seemed very nice by that stage!"

Colin Horton remembers the dress code included wearing ties. After a crawl around half a dozen pubs, he and his mates wondered how they'd get in. "Simple: we would buy a tie from someone, cut it in half so two could use it to get in. Happy days!"

Robin Moorcroft worked as a glass collector at the Locarno when he was doing 'A' levels. "The band would play on the giant revolving stage. At the end of their set they'd play 'Time is Tight' by Booker T & the MGs, which would be a cue

Pete Clemons, sporting the big hair look: 'Well, it was the 70s'

for the stage to revolve and the next band to emerge playing the same tune as if it were a seamless carousel. One of the bands was called White Rum, which people thought was exotic".

Rock legends Led Zeppelin played at the Locarno on December 9th, 1971, as part of their 'back to the clubs' tour. Ticket prices were meant to be low as a way of saying 'thank you' to fans. Coventry music writer Pete Clemons tells us many thought £1 was a "bit steep" when earlier gigs were only 75p!

Just as everything was rocking along, there was a bomb scare. Everyone was ordered out in the cold as the place was searched. The adoring 'Zep' fans were none too happy about this interruption but breathed a huge sigh of relief when the concert was allowed to continue.

The playlist included: 'Immigrant Song', 'Whole lotta Love' and of course the classic 'Stairway to Heaven': very apt for the Locarno!

Chuck Berry's live version of 'My-Ding-a-Ling' was recorded at the Locarno on February 3rd, 1972. First put down by Dave Bartholomew in 1952, it was re-recorded under different titles before Chuck reverted to the original. If you listen carefully to the recording, you

---

THE LANCHESTER POLYTECHNIC
COLLEGE ARTS FESTIVAL
(JAN 28th-FEB 4th)
PRIORY STREET, COVENTRY

PINK FLOYD
CHUCK BERRY
SLADE

VIV STANSHALL AND FRIENDS • THUNDERCLAP NEWMAN
LIGHTNIN' SLIM • J. B. HUTTO AND THE HAWKS
EDDIE 'GUITAR' BURNS • HOMESICK JAMES
ROLAND KIRK • MIKE WESTBROOK

ALSO EVENTS THROUGHOUT THE WEEK. TICKETS AND FULL PROGRAMME
AVAILABLE FROM THE COLLEGE AND USUAL AGENCIES

Locarno headliners Led Zeppelin

will catch the Coventry accents of the audience who were enthusiastically singing along!

Audience participation was a big part of his act and the song's double meanings were ramped up to the full. Chuck got the girls singing "my" and the boys singing "ding-a-ling", all very cheeky! He was one artist in a stellar cast that included Slade and Billy Preston, all part of the Lanchester Polytechnic's annual Arts Festival.

> Paul Sadler: **"I went to see Iggy Pop there, the punk icon as I had become a punk. The Rockhouse was the place to be for getting into fights over a girl or people knocking your beer over!"**

Coventry barber and music fan Paul Daly had wanted tickets for Pink Floyd but they were sold out. The "next best thing" was Chuck Berry. Paul remembers "Billy Preston was great, Slade got the audience going, so by the time Chuck came on he had them in his hands".

Pink Floyd's appearance made it even more mind-blowing after stepping in due to David Bowie pulling out. They treated the audience to an early version of their iconic album 'Dark Side of the Moon', with the working title of 'Eclipse'.

When they came on stage, the audience was enthralled as tracks such as 'Time and Money' were played. Pete Clemons says that it was soon very clear that they were listening to something "incredibly special". What a starry night at the Rockhouse!

Slade returned in May later that year to play to a packed crowd. Hailing from Walsall, they were almost local, with front man 'Noddy' Holder a working class lad who grew up in a council house, just as many Coventry kids did. The band played music people could sing-along to as well as dance to and always drew the crowds when they played.

Other top bands appearing include Judas Priest in August 1973 and Ultravox in September 1977. Siouxsie and the Banshees appeared in October 1977 and were back in October the next year along with Human League. Generation X played there in April 1978.

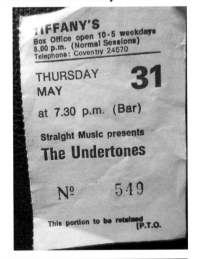

Siouxsie Sioux -
Photo: Pete Hill

The Clash Tiffanys 1979 Photo: Rob Lapworth

Heavy metal fan David Hayes was also partial to punk and went to the Clash gig in 1977. "Just as The Clash started their encore a glass or bottle tossed from somewhere bounced off me noggin leaving me unconscious for a few seconds and a permanent lump on the forehead." The Clash did a few more gigs at Tiff's as did other punk bands.

The Locarno was renamed Tiffany's in the late '70s. When local drummer John Hewitt wasn't playing a gig he went there on Tuesday nights with his friends. "I saw loads of bands there in the '70s, including XTC in 1978".

John D'Arcy saw the Pretenders around the end of 1979. "They weren't bad but the support band was absolutely superb! Unknowns at the time-UB40!"

Coventry's very own 2-Tone band the Specials immortalised the nightspot in their song, 'Friday Night, Saturday Morning'. The lyrics sum a night out there: girls dancing round their handbags, the crowded bar, bouncers keeping an eye out for trouble and people thinking "what am I doing here?"

In 1979 they recorded their 'Too Much Too Young' at the venue in front of a very enthusiastic audience. The Selecter also appeared there in front of their home crowd.

Local singer and global star Ray King retains a soft spot for the Locarno where he performed as well as having many good times with friends. "It was a big melting pot, everyone went there, black and white, to dance, to see famous bands".

After a few years as Tiffany's, this much-loved nightspot closed for good, re-opening in 1986 as the city's Central Library.

The Specials

Precinct with Locarno in the background

Specials Saturday Night, Sunday Morning on 2-Tone Mural

Tickets galore! (From John Coles collection)

MR GEORGE, GEORGE'S AND SOME SCARY PLACES

CHAPTER 3

George Hendry (far right) and colleagues at his nightclub

1972 and there's a new kid on the block - Mr George's. Dirty Stop Outs checked it out, liked what they saw and kept going back for more.

Entertainment entrepreneur George Hendry named the new nightspot after himself and why not? Hailing from Glasgow where he had made money from butcher shops and other businesses, he settled in Coventry and established some memorable venues.

Mike Lewis remembers him managing the casino and bingo hall on the Radford Road: "That was when they still made Jaguar cars at the nearby factory on Sandy Lane. After he left there, he opened George's nightclub."

George's, later Park Lane and then 'Mr G's', was conveniently located on the upper level of the Lower Precinct. The bouncers wore bow-ties and Colin Horton, a huge fan of the nightclub, remembers "what a nice bloke Ben the doorman was, always smiling. Who can forget the hot dogs on sticks?" Who indeed.

Colin Horton: **"I was there on the opening night and throughout the '70s. Saw the Drifters three nights running, Monday, Tuesday and Wednesday! Also Edwin Starr. Everyone knew everyone really. Christmas and New Year's Eve were great nights, so busy you just couldn't move. Best night was Sunday- half price drinks till 12!"**

MR. GEORGE

VALUE TICKET. Week Comm 9th January

	Scene 2	Scene 1
Mon 9th	New Wave From AUTOMATICS	Solid Gold Disco

20p admission with ticket till 10.00 pm
After 10.00 30p admission with ticket

Tues 10th Scene One – DISCO THRO TILL TWO
FREE admission with ticket
Scene Two available for private hire

| Wed 11th | Scene 2 Available for Private Hire | Scene 1 Disco Party Nite Super Disco 8pm till 2am |

| Thurs 12th | Scene 2 Heavy Rock From * MOTORHEAD * | Scene 1 Solid Gold Disco |

Ladies Free till 10pm...22p Drinks till 10 30pm

Fri 13th FANTASTIC DOUBLE DISCO NITE
20p Admission 22p Drinks Before 10pm
After 10pm Adm. Only 60p

Sat 14th NEW WAVE & PUNK ROCK
Scene 2 FROM The Lurkers & The Reaction
Scene 1 SUPER DISCO
The first 100 people admitted FREE

Sun 15th Scene 2 Scene 1
Sunday Disco Club Free Membership
Doors open 7.30pm...Drinks 22p All Nite
...Two available for private hire

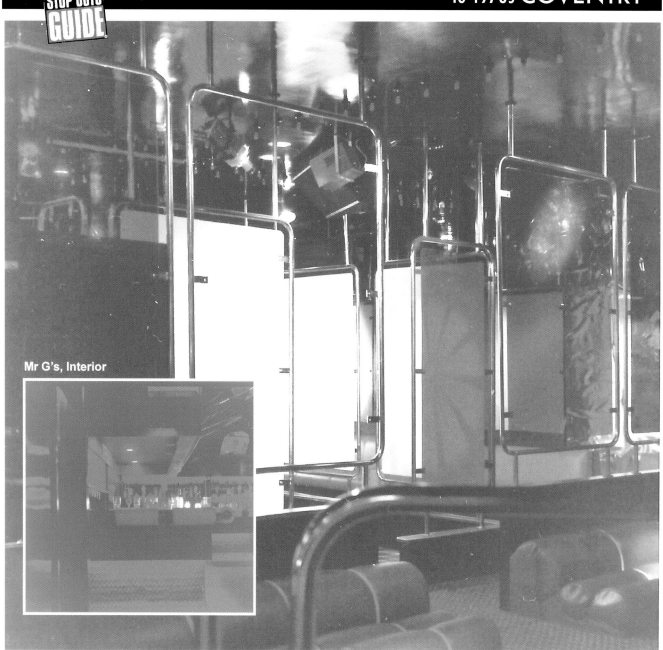

Mr G's, Interior

Mr G's, DJ box

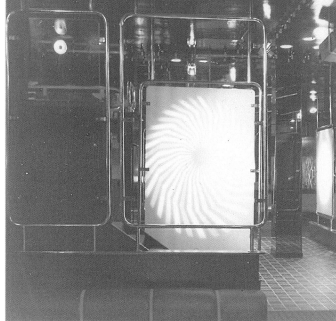

Hendry not only ran a top nightclub but also lived at the top, in the penthouse of the Precinct's Hillman House. He had an enviable view of his adopted city and entertainment empire.

Sherry Gorman lived in the same block. "I was on the 11th floor and there were only the two of us living there for many years, plus George's lovely wolfhound! It was great living there during my heydays with so many nightclubs and bars right on my doorstep!"

Many people enjoyed the 'Adam & Eve' themed Friday nights. Males were given a sticker with a name on

> Paul Sadler: **"Mr George's was a great place to hang out. It's where I first saw the Sex Pistols and became hooked."**

such as Adam or Anthony and were meant to find their famous matching partner. We can only guess how many romances, marriages and children resulted from these evenings.

The Coventry Telegraph described it at the time as being a "great way of getting the opposite sexes talking to each other".

Colin Horton liked George's so much that he'd sometimes sneak out of work to go there: "When I was my mate Gus's best man, I went to work at the Ryton car plant on the Thursday night, climbed over the fence after getting paid at 10pm and went straight to George's to join his stag night!"

Mr G's entrance, Upper floor, lower Precinct

George's offered variety, with bands old and new appearing. The start of October 1974 saw Heads Together offering 'funky music'. Entry was 45p for ladies, free before 9.30pm but 55p for men. Not quite equal opportunities but the idea was that having women there early would lure in the men earlier. Political correctness had yet to hit the nightclubs.

George's kept up with the latest musical trends and became a place for the emerging punk scene.

Thin Lizzy at Mr George's Photo: John Coles

MR GEORGE
LOWER PRECINCT COVENTRY

THE SEX PISTOLS

SATURDAY 17th DECEMBER 7.30 p.m.
Advance Tickets(£1.75) from Virgin
Records or the George Club

Miranda Aston rushed to get to the Sex Pistols gig

The Buzzcocks played there in October 1977 and so did the Vibrators.

Monday became punk night with local bands given a chance to show what they could do. Squad was one such band that formed in 1977, originally with Terry Hall on vocals.

The Sex Pistols gig at George's on December 17th, 1977, was one for the history books, being one of just a handful of gigs on the 'Never Mind the Bans' tour. The band's attitude, language, lyrics and style had upset many people but not George Hendry. He seized the opportunity to have them appear at his nightclub. Word spread like wildfire about the gig. Miranda Aston was phoned up by a friend that afternoon and told her name was on the door and to get to George's quickly. She did, arriving for the rehearsals and staying till the concert that evening.

What did she make of it all?

"They were quite good but as the day went on it went downhill a bit. They played much better in the rehearsals. It got very lively! Sid Vicious was bouncing off the wall. Definitely a never to be forgotten moment."

Johnny Rotten was happy to wind up the local crowd. He mentioned how his team, Arsenal, had won that day, whereas Coventry City had lost 2-1 at home. But Sex Pistols fans knew what to expect from the band.

Local musician John Hewitt managed to get a

precious ticket, one of 500. He actually put it in his shoe for safe keeping: "I was very impressed. But I thought they rushed their set and didn't play for the full time." Those remarks were apt, it was a shortened gig.

The Rhythm Doctor was also there and seeing the Sex Pistols was a real stand out moment for him.

This gig was one of the band's last in the UK before they set off for America and their ill-fated last tour.

Coventry band the Automatics took note of what was going on during the Sex Pistols gig. They were not on that evening's bill but probably would have liked to have been. They were soon to play there, as Mr George was nurturing the next music trend that would sweep across the country.

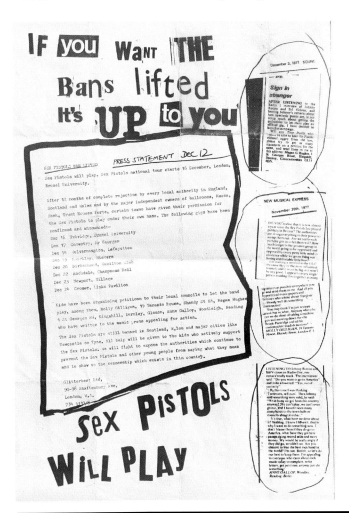

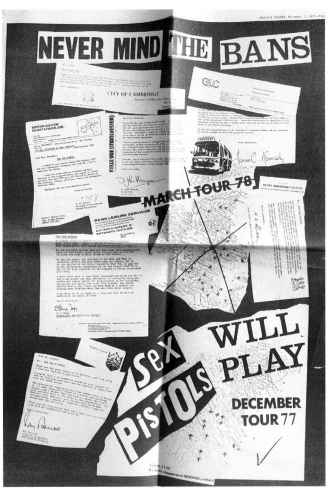

Colin Horton, a big fan of Mr George's

NIGHT CLUB & RESTAURANT
Cabaret, Dancing, Late Bar

TOP SPOT

7-8 BISHOP STREET, COVENTRY
Telephone: 26913/22995

Christmas and New Year celebrations were all a blurry memory by early January 1978. George's offered some respite by signing up the Automatics for a three-month residency. Part of the emerging 2-Tone music movement, it was a great place to trial it out. Just over a year later, the band were known as Special AKA.

George bought another Coventry nightclub, the Forty Thieves, setting aside £40,000 to convert it into a late-night Italian cabaret. Sherry Gorman had "loved the Forty Thieves" but, by this time, it had lost its magic

When two nightclubs ruled city's music scene

touch and gained a bit of a notoriety for the wrong reasons. George wanted to revive its fortunes so ditched the old name and it re-emerged as Sophia's in early 1974.

It later morphed into Busters and Albany barmaid Lizzi Maxsted had it on her list of go-to places.

"I loved reggae music and sometimes after work, on a weekend, I would go to a nightclub, mainly Busters, that played reggae, with a bit or funk and soul. I was only 16 but easily passed for older."

She sometimes went with a friend but didn't mind going on her own "to chill out with a double Southern Comfort and lemonade and a Mores Cigarette, to pose. I never inhaled the smoke!"

George Hendry's empire later expanded to London, Paris and Majorca. His company F and H famously bought the Hippodrome in Leicester Square, formerly owned by the flamboyant Peter Stringfellow.

When he died in 2008, aged 77, George was remembered as a local legend who gave our Dirty Stop Outs many memorable nights out and helped young bands to find their feet and develop their musical styles.

The top spot for the scariest nightclub in town would probably be awarded to... the Top Spot! It didn't get rave reviews in the Coventry Telegraph's survey of the city's former nightclubs.

"It seemed to terrify you all in equal measure, with many saying they had only frequented the club just once."

Colin Horton: **"The Top Spot! That takes me back. We only went there if we got knocked back from the Locarno. Rough as old boots but cheap and full of characters."**

It was viewed as being more for the over 30s who are always scary to the younger generation. John D'Arcy went there "occasionally" and felt relaxed, possibly because the doormen were friends of his parents and kept an eye out for him.

John Starkey used to go there and said it could a bit rough sometimes. He got on the wrong side of a big guy one night just for waving at the woman he was dancing with - she was actually his friend...

Local singer Sue Starr went to the Top Spot one evening and survived unscathed but possibly because she ended up at the Pink Parrot over in Tower Street: "One of my friends bumped into a guy she recognised from her school days. He told her he was the owner of the Top Spot and the Pink Parrot. We all thought he was just talking a load of bull, but to prove he wasn't, he took all of us over there. His office had a view out

Gillian Dawson: **"You went to the Top Spot at your peril if you looked like a student! Still managed a few good nights there though."**

over the nightclub. We were treated as VIP guests, no expense spared. We had a great night!"

Opened in 1974, the popular Pink Parrot was owned by Johnny O'Brien and his family and went through various names and images. Many will recall it as the City Centre Club, a venue Pete Clemons saw was in head-to-head competition with George's. Many top names appeared there to rival those appearing at George's and the Locarno. It ended up being refurbished and renamed Tamango's.

Sue Lowe ended up at Tamango's on her Hen Night in September 1977. "It's the only memory I have of the place. Yes, we danced in a circle with our handbags in the middle and I seem to remember having a cocktail or two!"

Wonder if they served her the 'real' Tamango cocktails? This Italian ruby-red concoction was known for its high alcohol content and hallucinogenic qualities.

The Pink Parrot

NEVER MIND THE BANS

SEX WILL PISTOLS PLAY

DECEMBER TOUR 77

ANARCHY IN THE U.K.

DEC 17

COVENTRY

MR GEORGES

£1.75

7.30 P.M.

GETTING AN ALL-ROUND DIRTY STOP OUT EDUCATION

There's no doubt Coventry offered a pretty impressive roster of partying opportunities in the 1970s for its student population.

They flocked to gigs and dances at the city's higher education institutions, including the 'Lanch' (Lanchester Polytechnic.) Its Student Union stood across the road from the cathedral and had its own claim to fame, being at the cutting-edge of 1970s music trends. Much of the action started off in the Sports Hall where keeping fit was the last thing on people's minds.

> Pete Clemons: **"The Lanch was pivotal in promoting 1970s musical trends. You couldn't over-emphasise how important this venue was when bands were taking their music up and down the country."**

Teenagers mixed with Lanch students - the latter being a few years older seemed "really cool" to their more youthful counterparts. After finishing her shift at the Round Café, Gill Dawson headed to the less mainstream nightspots such as the Lanch. Aged 15, she preferred progressive and punk line-ups. Gill saw the Sex Pistols there and went to the sell-out concerts of Hawkwind, Pink Floyd, Genesis and Roxy Music.

The Lanch Arts Festivals were legendary, sell-out events though they usually ran at a loss. Social secretary Ted Little was one of the main organisers helping to get the festival going in 1970.

In January 1971 ticket requests 'pouring in' to the Arts Festival office. Within two days, they sold £1000 worth

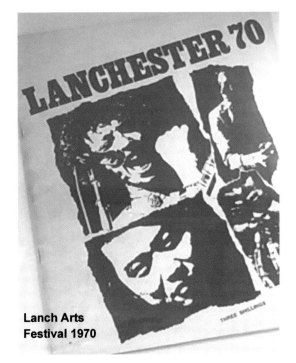

Lanch Arts Festival 1970

of tickets- not bad considering there were no internet sales then. The ten-day £12,000 festival's focus was very much on music and poetry.

In the festival line up were: Ronnie Scott, Ralph McTell and the Strawbs. A ticket for Elton and Caravan playing in the Main Hall cost 16 shillings. Other bands that played there included T Rex, Free and The Who.

The Clash and Sex Pistols both played there on November 29th, 1976. Punk rock was spitting and pogoing its way into the headlines so the Lanch organisers took a risk and booked them.

Student Union President Phil Dunn described it politely as a very "intense" evening. The Clash preceded the Sex Pistols. He said: "Strummer with blond hair and paint-spattered army fatigues, Mick Jones in Union Jack shirt and black tie, Paul Simonon looking cool as always in red graffiti white shirt and tie and Terry Chimes in red shirt."

This was the first live rendition of The Sex Pistols' 'God Save the Queen' under its working title 'No Future'. It was a gig to remember

Lanch Arts Festival 1974 programme

...pearance of Soft Machine at Warwick this week, is to a large ...a response to the demand for "Big Name"...

Left: Hand-made poster by Chris Long advertising his 2nd session DJing at the Lanch
Above: Soft Machine review

Students occupy the Lanch admin building

Sue Lowe: **"I saw my first live band at the Lanch, Steppenwolf, in 1972. I don't think our parents were even aware that we'd been going there!"**

or forget, depending on your nervous disposition. It was just days before the band's infamous Sex Pistols TV interview with Bill Grundy who asked them to say something outrageous. They obliged, triggering hundreds of 'shock horror' headlines and instant fame!

Steve Connelly, known as Scon to many, helped the Sex Pistols load their equipment that night. He soon joined them and the Clash, as the roadie, taking on the fitting punk name of Roadent. His friend Trev Teasdel says: "Roadent later said that those bohemian days in Coventry were good training for life on the road with those bands. Who knew it was work experience!" Going to the Lanch that night helped him get a job.

The Lanch also inadvertently brought together some musicians who left their mark on the world. Horace Panter came to Coventry in 1972 to study fine art and met Jerry Dammers. They went on to be two founding

Gill Dawson: **"If I missed the bus, I thought nothing of walking home in my maxi skirt and flip-flops. I'd just hitch up my long skirt, the height of fashion then, and walk quickly homeward!"**

members of The Specials. The Lanch was later used as the setting for the video of their 'Rat Race' single. Nick

Edgington reckons this song was 'taking the piss' out of the posh students!

A late-night bus service was provided for revellers, doing a circular route around the suburbs. This was handy for those who missed the last bus from Pool Meadow because they were lost in music or in someone's arms.

Phil Dunn: **"It was the days of tuxedoed, bow-tied security men who could be a bit tasty. They were confronted by all these punks in bondage strides, ripped T-shirts and chains. As tension built, the band came on. The atmosphere was pretty electric with wild pogoing. It felt like the coming of something, an event."**

It was lively atmosphere on the bus, lots of laughs, banter and even a last chance for romance. Some people missed their stop and ended walking home. Gill Dawson remembers it going down her street and her mum being a bit annoyed because it woke up the neighbours.

Local bands also regularly played at the Lanch such as The Wild Boys and The Urge.

Tickets from John Coles collection

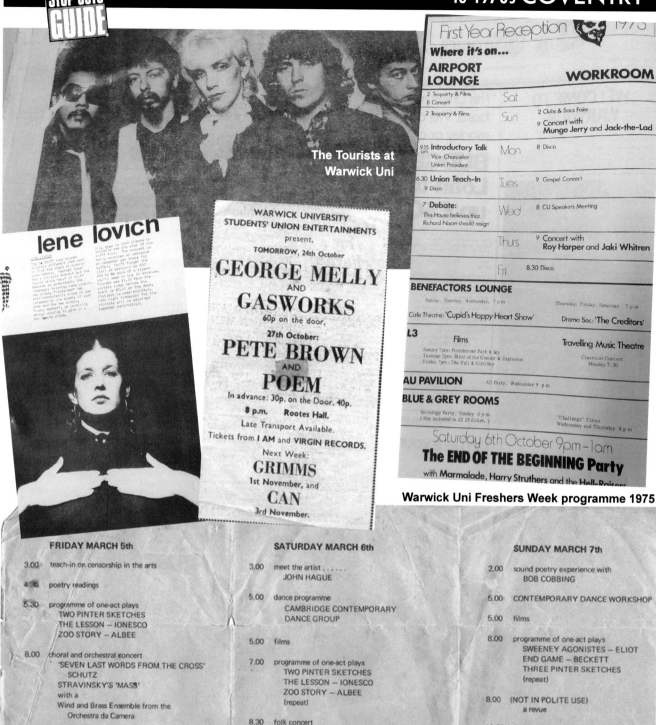

The Tourists at Warwick Uni

lene lovich

WARWICK UNIVERSITY STUDENTS' UNION ENTERTAINMENTS present,

TOMORROW, 24th October

GEORGE MELLY AND GASWORKS

60p on the door.

27th October:

PETE BROWN AND POEM

In advance: 30p, on the Door, 40p.

8 p.m.   Rootes Hall.

Late Transport Available.

Tickets from I AM and VIRGIN RECORDS.

Next Week:

GRIMMS

1st November, and

CAN

3rd November.

First Year Reception 1975

Where it's on...

AIRPORT LOUNGE — **WORKROOM**

2 Teaparty & Films / 8 Concert	Sat	
2 Teaparty & Films	Sun	2 Clubs & Socs Faire / 9 Concert with Mungo Jerry and Jack-the-Lad
9.15 am Introductory Talk / Vice-Chancellor / Union President	Mon	8 Disco
6.30 Union Teach-In / 9 Disco	Tues	9 Gospel Concert
7 Debate: / This House believes that Richard Nixon should resign	Wed	8 CU Speakers Meeting
	Thurs	9 Concert with Roy Harper and Jaki Whitren
	Fri	8.30 Disco

BENEFACTORS LOUNGE

Sunday, Tuesday, Wednesday, 7 p m   Thursday, Friday, Saturday, 7 p m

Cafe Theatre: 'Cupid's Happy Heart Show'   Drama Soc: 'The Creditors'

L3 Films — Travelling Music Theatre

Sunday 7pm: Punishment Park & Ice / Tuesday 7pm: Blod of the Condor & Explosion / Friday 7pm: The Fall & Girl/Boy — Classical Concert Monday 7.30

AU PAVILION — AU Party, Wednesday 9 p m

BLUE & GREY ROOMS

Sociology Party, Sunday 8 p m — "Challenge" Films Wednesday and Thursday 8 p m
(Not included in £2 25 ticket.)

Saturday 6th October 9pm–1am

The END OF THE BEGINNING Party

with Marmalade, Harry Struthers and the Hell-Raisers

Warwick Uni Freshers Week programme 1975

FRIDAY MARCH 5th

3.00 teach-in on censorship in the arts

4.30 poetry readings

5.30 programme of one-act plays
TWO PINTER SKETCHES
THE LESSON – IONESCO
ZOO STORY – ALBEE

8.00 choral and orchestral concert
'SEVEN LAST WORDS FROM THE CROSS' SCHUTZ
STRAVINSKY'S 'MASS'
with a
Wind and Brass Ensemble from the Orchestra da Camera

8.00 programme of one-act plays
SWEENEY AGONISTES – ELIOT
END GAME – BECKETT
THREE PINTER SKETCHES

10.00 blues workshop concert
EDGAR BROUGHTON BAND
HIGH TIDE
INDIAN SUMMER
SORROWS

LATE BAR
LATE TRANSPORT

WARWICK ARTS FESTIVAL

SATURDAY MARCH 6th

3.00 meet the artist . . . . . .
JOHN HAGUE

5.00 dance programme
CAMBRIDGE CONTEMPORARY DANCE GROUP

5.00 films

7.00 programme of one-act plays
TWO PINTER SKETCHES
THE LESSON – IONESCO
ZOO STORY – ALBEE
(repeat)

8.30 folk concert
JEREMY TAYLOR
JO-ANNE KELLY
APRIL

12.00 (NOT IN POLITE USE)
a revue

1.00 films

throughout the festival:

FILM HAPPENINGS with CAROLEE SCHNEEMAN
JOHN HAGUE – an exhibition of work
'INSITE' – an arts magazine
exhibitions of:
POETRY BY LOCAL SCHOOL CHILDREN
POSTERS
PHOTOGRAPHY

UNIVERSITY OF WARWICK Rootes Hall

SUNDAY MARCH 7th

2.00 sound poetry experience with
BOB COBBING

5.00 CONTEMPORARY DANCE WORKSHOP

5.00 films

8.00 programme of one-act plays
SWEENEY AGONISTES – ELIOT
END GAME – BECKETT
THREE PINTER SKETCHES
(repeat)

8.00 (NOT IN POLITE USE)
a revue

10.00 blues workshop concert
SKIN ALLEY
PINK FAIRIES
BUBASTIS
ASGARD
WHISTLER
(and friends)

tickets from:

UNIVERSITY OF WARWICK
or by post from
'FESTIVAL'
FIELDGATE CLOSE
FIELDGATE LANE
KENILWORTH
tel KENILWORTH 55487

WEEKEND INCLUSIVE TICKET 10/-

Warwick Arts Festival programme 1971

Nick Edgington: **"The 'Rat Race' video was filmed in the Lanch Sports Hall. I was a student there and it was cool seeing it on the telly. And one of the lyrics mentioned the "sacred college scarf", which I wore with pride at the time."**

Over at Warwick University, they were running their own festivals. Trev Teasdel says: "They were truly multi-media with street theatre, absurdist plays, sound poetry in and around the social block, progressive, folk and blues bands and artists over the weekend and so much more." Trev remembers doing his first poetry reading there in Airport lounge with the Umbrella Poets in 1971.

There was an impressive roll-call of bands over the decade: Al Stewart, Soft Machine, Roy Harper, Caravan, Desmond Dekker and many more.

After Warwick's Arts Centre opened in 1974, it became an important venue, attracting audiences not just from across Coventry but further afield. The official opening looked in danger of not happening due to student protests. The seventies - as we know - was immortalised by industrial action and they started early it seems!

Nick Edgington's first gig at Warwick was Lene Lovich. "'I think we must have gone in a friend's car, as it was a bit out of town." The singer had several hits including 'Lucky Number' in 1979 and appeared at Warwick twice that year.

Stuart Beamish didn't think she was very good at all but a review in Warwick's student newspaper The Boar wrote that she was "excellent" and "one of few women who can actually hold a band together".

The Tourists, whose members included Annie Lennox

Friday, 5th March, 1971
Edgar Broughton Band
High Tide
Indian Summer
Sorrows

UMBRELLA POETS 8 PM AIRPORT LOUNGE

Sunday, 7th March, 1971
Pink Fairies
Skin Alley
Bubastis
Asgard
Tunc

At University of Warwick Rootes Hall
INCLUSIVE FESTIVAL WEEKEND TICKET 10/-

and Dave Stewart, played at Warwick in 1979.

Canley Teachers' Training College had an active Student Union that brought the likes of Status Quo, Genesis, Average White Band and Fairport Convention to campus. Martin Barker saw Procol Harum and Trapeze at Canley but says he mostly went to the Lanch, where he saw "too many to mention!"

Rag week procession

JIM, TERRY, DAVE & PETE are....

WALRUS GUMBOOT

Coventry Technical College was a classical style building in the Butts, near the city centre. Opened in 1935, it was still educating and entertaining students in the '70s. The power cuts of 1974 meant they were restricted to just one dance a term. They made it a good one with Walrus Gumboot and Glade Sounds disco.

Coventry Technical College Students' Section

President: Alan Moxon
Vice-President, Internal: Jane Conning
Vice-President, External: Jimmy Anderson
Hon. Secretary: Celia Millhouse
Hon. Treasurer: R. W. Watts

Technical College,
Butts,
Coventry,
CV1 3GD.
Telephone: Coventry 57221 Ext. 277
(S.T.D. 0203)

Dear Trev,
Owing to the present power crisis, Cov Tech Ents Committee are only allowed one dance this term, but it's gonna be a goodie! We've got Glade Sounds Disco and no-one less than THE "WALRUS GUMBOOT"!!

So what Iwas wondering was whether youcould possibly advertise this on your free ads page in HOBO if you're publishing onebefore Friday March the 1st. If so, here is the info:

Friday March 1st at 8.oop.m. till late,

In the Refectory, Albany Road, Earlsdon, Coventry,

Cov Tech Ents Committee proudly present the return of

WALRUS GUMBOOT.
+
GLADE SOUNDS DISCO.

There will be a late bar for those interested!

Cov Tech College ents information

Henley College held a regular folk club at the New Inn, Longford. Trev Teasdel remembers his art teacher Barry Jackson who he describes as "a legend". He could play 12 instruments of the ancient folk variety. Along with fellow lecturer Roland Matthews they ran folk band – Folklore - and made an album produced by Coventry folk radio presenter Norman Wheatley. Trev himself later played floor spots at Henley Folk club.

Gaining an all-round nightlife education extended right across Coventry. Students and non-students joined in the fun and made the most of all that was on offer with plenty of gigs, discos and festivals.

COV. TECH. ENTS. COMMITTEE 160

presents the return of

Walrus Gumboot
Glade Sounds Disco

FRIDAY MARCH 1

8 till late, good lights

Guests 25p

Coventry Technical College, the Butts

DISCO FEVER! SILK AT THE BEAR, DJs AND DANCING JUST ABOUT EVERYWHERE

CHAPTER 5

sunshine

CRAIG WARD
entertainment consultants
suppliers of p.a.
and discotheque equipment
132 gulson road coventry CV1 2JF
telephone 0203 - 23020 ...

At THE WALSGRAVE
Tuesday June 23rd
PETE WATERMAN PRESENTS
A
HEAVY CONCERT
with
: WANDERING JOHN
PANTOMIME
Tickets 2/-
Come early !

Above: Sunshine Entertainment, Craig Ward's card and Walsgrave ticket

Left: Disco girl Liz Smith, aged 17, with fab dancing shoes!

Disco fever was breaking out across Coventry long before John Travolta appeared on the silver screen. Dirty stop outs trekked from one end of the city to the other to try out their moves. Most pubs ran discos so the sound of loud music blasting out was normal as was dancing round handbags.

The Walsgrave was an out-of-town pub pulling in the crowds, Liz Smith among them. "They had a great disco in the '70s, me and my friends used to go there a lot."

Colin Horton: **"The Walsgrave had a disco and bands on Tuesdays, like Wandering John. The lead singer used to wear long yellow boots."**

Annette Williscroft: **"A lot of smaller pubs in the suburbs started to have discos or bands. The Baginton Oak was the first to use some sort of fluorescent lighting so if you wore white you glowed in the dark. Even your underwear would show through your clothes. Dandruff was a problem!"**

THE BAGINTON OAK
"COSMIC MUSIC CLUB"
Presents
This Wednesday—
A modern jazz/rock night with
"WAVE"
and supporting discs!
8-11 p.m. Direct Enterprises.
Next Week: PATSY POWELL.

STEAM PACKET

At the "Top Live Bands" EVERY Sunday

TREE TOPS

Sounds of Venus Disco

FOLESHILL ROAD. CLUB.

NEW ROCK VENUE

SUNDAYS

8 till late bar - 35p/25 - students.

Tree Tops Club Steam Packet flyer

Spinning the discs there one night a week was the ubiquitous Pete Waterman. The disco craze led to an explosion in DJing as a nice little earner, even a 'proper' career for some.

Becoming a DJ

Pete Waterman grew up in the Coventry's Stoke Heath district and his career as a DJ sort of happened by chance. A former British Rail steam locomotive fireman, his passion for railways never faded. He tried his hand at grave digging before working at Coventry's GEC plant in the mid-1960s. He gigged in a band called Tomorrow's Kind a few nights a week but wasn't convinced of his talent for that. When another band failed to show up at a gig in 1966, Pete rushed home to get his record box and played them instead.

The pub's landlord and customers really liked it, so he was asked back again for the fee of ten bob. Pete Waterman remembers: "By a quirk of fate, I went from being lead singer in a not very good band to being the only DJ in Coventry. I began to play records more than I played instruments."

Sue Long: **"Lots of lovely memories of The Plough on the London Road and all that was going on there as well."**

Trev Teasdel sometimes worked at the Walsgrave's progressive music night. "Tuesdays, doors opened 8pm but I'd get there early to help Pete and the band set up."

Colin Horton spotted Pete at few times. "I was a schoolboy at Caludon Castle School and he was working at the GEC. I'd see him on the bus going to the Walsgrave with his little box of records."

There must have been magic in that 'little box' as DJ Pete became more in demand and eventually a pivotel figure in the music business.

Liz Smith: **"We had some great nights at the Tree Tops Club!"**

COVENTRY SOUL CLUB moves to the TREE TOPS CLUB, Foleshill Road, Thursday, 4th October, 8 till midnight, with PETE WATERMAN playing all of the great Soul sounds, First Night FREE. Nov. 8th: J. J. BARNES.

Over in Foleshill, the Tree Tops Club was bringing in the crowds. On Thursdays, it was Pete Waterman once again spinning the discs at the Soul Club. Monday's Apollo Club was more rock oriented, with a 'heavy' disco. Entry: 55p, 25p for students.

John Willcox had his first taste of DJing at the local youth club in Styvechale. He then moved on to pubs, including the popular Climax, in the late '70s. He supported the bands that played there also spun the discs at the Zodiac on Whitefriars Lane and occasionally the Swanswell Tavern.

"I can't remember exactly how I started DJing at the Climax or the Zodiac! I'm guessing that I went to see

Young DJ Pete Waterman

bands there and there wasn't a DJ so I just volunteered my services for the next gig! I just turned up with my homemade set of decks, some records and plugged in to the PA and played music before, between and after the bands. I very rarely got paid but I wasn't doing it for a living, luckily! I just enjoyed playing records."

DJ John Willcox

MORE THANJUSTA DISCO 8-12 POLYTECH DOWNSTAIRS BAR PUNK DUB ROCKERS SOUL MOVERS??????? WEDNESDAY 5th APR NO MANNERS REQUIRED

Chris Long's DIY poster for his 1st Lanch gig

DJ John Willcox still spinning the discs! Photo: Martin Ward

It was at the Climax where he got the moniker of Johnny Cocaine.

"I was talking to Johnny 'Wild Boy' Thompson at the end of a gig when Dave Gedney of the Edge joined us. He knew Johnny, but not me and asked "who are you then?" I told him my name and he said 'we've already got Johnny Wildboy, so you're' as he looked at my 'Enjoy Cocaine' T-shirt, 'Johnny Cocaine!' I liked it and kept using it."

Where did John acquire this distinctive T-shirt? "My mum bought it for me one day when she went on a works outing to the coast somewhere. She thought it was funny. My dad hated it. I was a 17-year-old at the time and didn't even really know what cocaine was."

He bought a couple more iron on transfers, "as used on all T-shirts back then" and put them on the front of his disco speakers to become Cocaine Discos. He used to play Dillinger's 'Cocaine in My Brain' track a lot too. "I'd probably played it that night I was 'christened'!"

The very first record he played at the Climax was 'New Rose' by the Damned. "I remember it clearly because I had it lined up and was waiting for the support band to end. A girl came up to me, not seeing what I had ready to go, and asked, 'Have you got anything by the Damned?' I proudly pointed to the record I was about to play. There were still a few minutes to go before the band ended and we got talking about music. On the strength of my first record choice we became good friends."

Chris Long's love of vinyl began very young. "I'd been collecting music since I was six years old! Dave Clark 5, 'My Boy Lollipop' (Millie Small), 'They're Coming to Take me Away' (Jerry Samuels) that sort of thing were in my early collection."

Wild Boy Johnnie Thompson in the news

"By the end of the night they did not seem to know what they were doing. The drummer was flaked out. It was disgusting."

Band too wild for junior disco

Evening Telegraph Reporter

COVENTRY punk band The Wild Boys lived up to their name during a disco-theque.

The group angered the organisers of a junior disco at Exhall East Community Centre, by drinking before and during their performance.

By the end of the night the centre committee claims, they were incapable of loading their own equipment, their driver refused to take them, and a taxi had to be ordered to get them home.

Marilyn Simpson, chairman of the centre committee, said: "They infuriated us by drinking on stage because we have a strict no-alcohol rule at our discos which are for 12-to-16-year-olds.

"By the end of the night they did not seem to know what they were doing. The

The Wild Boys' lead guitarist and vocalist, Johnny Thompson.

drummer was flaked out. It was disgusting."

Mrs Simpson said that before the group played she saw the four members with drinks in a back room. When she told them that she didn't want them to go on stage drunk, they said they usually had a drink to relax.

Paul Vuckovic, manager of the Wild Boys — Mark Byers, Tony Lynch, Johnny Thompson and Gary Cox — said the D.J. had told him the next day what had happened.

Left: DJ Johnnie Cocaine's logo

By the age of 12 he was already playing 'danceable pop music' in clubs. He added 'Tighten Up' volumes 2 and 3, 'Motown Chartbusters' and a host of soul and reggae hits to his collection. "Then it was jazz, rock, disco and funk, Santana's 'Abraxas', Roxy Music's first album and Hendrix.'

When Chris went to study fine art at the Lanch in 1978 a sense of dissatisfaction was the big catalyst for his DJing career. "I turned up at the Freshers Ball and heard only heavy metal. That was a big shock!"

The next day he went to the social secretary to ask for his own night where he could play his reggae and punk records. "At first he refused but I pestered him every week until he agreed!"

From then on Chris's DJ career grew and he became known as the Rhythm Doctor. He's still playing good tunes all these years later.

But it wasn't just the guys spinning the discs. Teenager Miranda Aston broke down some stereotypes when she started DJing at the Rose and Crown pub in the late '70s. It was a popular gay pub and had become punk friendly after initially turning them away when the style first took off. Miranda was a big punk fan and went to many gigs so knew the music and bands very well.

> Trev Teasdel: **"Friday nights were often spent at the Colin Campbell for the Village Heavy Rock club and disco. Local musician Al Docker and I used to go and then head to the Umbrella to continue the night."**

For prog rock, the Village venue upstairs at the Colin Campbell in Whitefriars Street was the place to go, with DJs such as Melv Preece and the Crazy Fox disco. It was just opposite the former Arts School, as the 'Lanch' once was and had been an important part of the Coventry music scene for years.

Warwick University's Tuesday night discos were just 15p to get in and Sue Long had some fun there. Aged 16, she started working at Barclays on the campus

He started young! 12 year-old Chris Long

and "went to pretty much everything that was on for the next four years!" A highlight she remembers is one night when she and her friend were the last ones standing after a disco in Warwick's Airport Lounge. "We were dancing over the tables and everywhere else to 'Silver Machine' by Hawkwind. Great times!'

THE VILLAGE
above Colin Campbell Whitefriars St.
(opposite Art College)

Friday 18th Dec.	Boots
Saturday 19th	Ra Ho Tep
Monday 21st	Heavy Disco
Christmas Eve	Surprise Rock Party (LATE BAR)
Boxing Night	April (LATE BAR)
New Years Eve	Fancy Dress-Prizes (LATE)
Friday 1st Jan	Children
Saturday 2nd	Junkhouse
Monday 4th	Heavy Disco
Friday 8th	Asgard
Saturday 9th	Power House
Monday 11th	Heavy Disco
Friday 15th	Indian Summer
Saturday 16th	Gentle (LATE BAR)
Monday 18th	Heavy Disco
Friday 22nd	Trad B. Jefferson
Saturday 23rd	Mead
Monday 25th	Heavy Disco
Friday 29th	Flight (LATE BAR)
Saturday 30th	Fresh Maggots

Coming in February - Duster Bennett
April 73 Fision.

The Village at the Colin Campbell pub listings

DJ Miranda and friend, Rose and Crown

Pure concentration! Miranda Aston DJing at the Rose and Crown

One of the Lanch DJs was a certain Dave Nellist who later became a longstanding Labour MP. Dave was not only radical in his politics but also his music, playing what he thought people needed to hear even if they didn't want to. Gill Dawson recalls him saying: "I'm going to f**king play it anyway!"

Sue Long was one of many followers of Silk Disco, a popular Coventry outfit co-founded by Jim Twyneham, Paul Taylor and Graham Wood. Craig Ward knew Graham well as he was a partner in the Sunshine Agency. "Happy days!", says Craig.

Sue Long went out with Graham Wood many moons ago. DJ Jim was quite a character and drove with a personalized number plate- '51LKO.' Turns out that his day job at that time was working at the Vehicle Licensing Office in Greyfriars Lane so that probably helped...

Silk Disco played all over Coventry but is often linked to the Bear Inn. Sue Lowe loved it from the outset in 1974. "Me and my friends saw an advert in the Coventry Evening Telegraph for a rock disco upstairs at the Bear Inn starting on Friday 1st February. We went on that first night."

They didn't tell their parents they were going and Sue can still remember the nervous excitement they shared as the bus turned into Broadgate. Also the very steep, narrow stairs, the small room with a bar on one side and stage on another.

Sue Long 1979

Silk disco in action

SILK DISCOTHEQUE
and Light Show

Nice work if
you can get it!
Silk disco DJ
Graham Wood

Silk disco DJ getting some record advice!

Sue Lowe: "The DJs had positioned themselves on the raised stage and the only illumination came from the disco lights and strobes scattered around the room. Led Zeppelin boomed out of the speakers and we were intoxicated by being in such a wild and, to us, dangerous place."

It turned out to be a night to remember in many ways. "That first Bear disco was when I met my future husband! He was 18, tall, dark and handsome, working for the GEC as a trainee telecommunications engineer, and from Yorkshire."

Brian was part of a group of lads who had been 'sent to Coventry' for training and were having "an amazing time", says Sue. "They all lived at the YMCA in the city centre. Most of them were 17 or 18, the first time they'd lived away from home."

Gill Dawson also went to the Bear. "DJ Jim looked like Rick Wakeman. We all fancied him, of course!" Sue Lowe was too busy fancying her husband-to-be though. The disco on Fridays was so popular that they started another rock disco on Saturday evenings and a Motown session on Sundays.

The much-fancied SILK disco DJ Jim Twyneham

Sue Lowe: "For several months we all went to the Bear on Friday and Saturday nights and some of us also used to go to Sunday's Motown discos, completely changing our 'rock chick' personas into a more conventional image."

John Coles of SILK famous jacket! Photo: John Coles

Tony Unwin: "Jim Twyneham was the king of Silk Disco back in the '70s. A drinking buddy of mine at the Styvechale Arms and good bloke to go with to watch the Sky Blues."

Sue Lowe remembers some real characters including a pair of curly haired lads who were 'absolutely mad' on The Who. "They modelled themselves on Roger Daltry and would 'air guitar' like crazy every time the DJs played anything by their heroes. People were so impressed that the floor would automatically clear for them."

In the early 1980s The Bear was demolished to make way for a bank. Even now, every time Sue walks past it, she remembers "that dark, smoky upstairs room, with its flashing strobes and ultraviolet lights flickering over a heaving mass of teenagers shaking their hair and playing air guitar to Deep Purple, Black Sabbath and the rest".

Disco fever meant that people could not only enjoy dancing but could earn a living from it. Many were keen to get in on the act as DJs, whilst holding down a day job. The equipment was often basic and so was the marketing - hand-written business cards became commonplace. It was the era of the mobile disco with part time DJs packing up their equipment into small vans and getting booked for weddings and birthdays and more.

Disco fever cooled down but never really went away. Dirty Stop Outs from '70s' Coventry are still (dis)gracing dance floors and DJs still playing good '70s sounds!

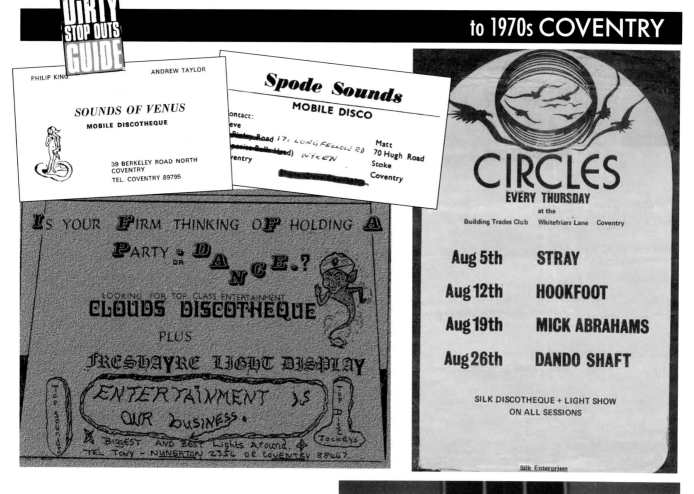

PHILIP KING   ANDREW TAYLOR

SOUNDS OF VENUS

MOBILE DISCOTHEQUE

39 BERKELEY ROAD NORTH
COVENTRY
TEL. COVENTRY 89795

Spode Sounds

MOBILE DISCO

Contact:
Steve   Matt
Bishop Road 17, LONGFELLOW RD   70 Hugh Road
(opposite Bulls Head) WYKEN   Stoke
Coventry   Coventry
Phone Dave Coventry

Is YOUR FIRM THINKING OF HOLDING A
PARTY or DANCE?
LOOKING FOR TOP CLASS ENTERTAINMENT
CLOUDS DISCOTHEQUE
PLUS
FRESHAYRE LIGHT DISPLAY
ENTERTAINMENT IS OUR BUSINESS.
BIGGEST AND BEST LIGHTS AROUND.
TEL TONY - NUNEATON 2354 OR COVENTRY 88447

CIRCLES

EVERY THURSDAY

at the
Building Trades Club   Whitefriars Lane   Coventry

Aug 5th	**STRAY**
Aug 12th	**HOOKFOOT**
Aug 19th	**MICK ABRAHAMS**
Aug 26th	**DANDO SHAFT**

SILK DISCOTHEQUE + LIGHT SHOW
ON ALL SESSIONS

Silk Enterprises

**Their eyes met across the crowded dancefloor!
Sue and Brian Lowe**

**From the disco to the church - Sue and Brian Lowe on their
wedding day, 1977**

COVENTRY THEATRE'S BOUNCING BALCONY, ZIGGY STARDUST TO THE RESCUE AND SPARKLING WINE AT THE BELGRADE

CHAPTER 6

Deep Purple- who nearly brought Coventry Theatre's balcony down!

The feeling of the earth moving under their feet was common with fans watching bands at the Coventry Theatre. The place rocked to the pulsating sounds of Deep Purple, David Bowie, Queen and many more in the era.

Local singer Sue Starr was at the Thin Lizzy gig in November 1976: "I was in the dress circle when I thought I was going to end up in the stalls below - the balcony was shaking so much with everybody head banging. I thought it was going to collapse! But a great night even though my ears were ringing the next day."

Gill Dawson experienced this sensation at a Deep Purple concert as did Stuart Beamish. "When they came back on for the encore it was definitely moving. This was their first concert in 1971. The second time the support band was Nazareth, who we'd never heard of".

Deep Purple played at the theatre several times in the early 70s.

Coventry Theatre had a capacity of 2,000 people and was made of sturdy stuff. Opened in 1937 as the New

Hippodrome, it was renamed the Coventry Theatre in 1955. It survived war time bombs, head bangers and heavy metal bands – it was definitely built to last.

Rescued by Bowie/Ziggy

The theatre kept up with the fast-moving '70s with most big names appearing. Gill Dawson went to see David Bowie in June 1973, part of the Ziggy Stardust tour. Many Bowie wannabes queued outside eagerly clutching their tickets, pleased as punch to be looking like they were from another planet.

For Sue Long it was the night that Ziggy Stardust came to her rescue.

"I was on the front row, as my neighbour worked in the box office and got tickets for me as soon as they went on sale. At the interval, I went to the bar and was slightly late coming back to my seat. I ran down the aisle, only to be caught by a security guard who grabbed me. David stopped the show and told them to let me go - what a night! I'll never forget it."

In 1973 Grease was already the word – in Coventry at any rate. A young American actor made his stage debut at Coventry Theatre as Danny Zuko in the rock 'n' roll musical – a few years before John Travolta played the role in the smash hit film. Who was this 23 year-old, relatively unknown actor? The one and only Richard Gere.

He understudied the show in America before being offered the lead in the original UK stage production. The rehearsals were in London before the show opened in Coventry in May 1973. From there it transferred to the West End.

The musical's programme wrote that Richard had "rocked all the way from the Broadway show". Coventry audiences loved it but there's no pleasing the critics. The Coventry Telegraph critic, David Isaacs, was not impressed, writing "what a waste of talent"! He wasn't just referring to Richard Gere but the whole acting pool.

From box office to corner shop

A small but perfectly formed place was the Poster Place, formerly the box office at Coventry Theatre. Thousands of youngsters and not so young-sters spent time there rummaging around for that special poster, badge or other bit of band memorabilia. The owners, Geoff Robinson and wife Janet, offered a veritable treasure trove in their shop.

Janet was a former performer at the theatre who once appeared in pantomime with Ken Dodd. She spotted the potential of the old box office. They kept up to date with the '70s rapidly changing tastes, from Bowie to the Bay City Rollers, punk and 2-Tone.

Miranda Aston was a big fan of the little shop and went there for any new punk badges and posters they had in.

The theatre's name was changed in 1979 to the Apollo, but its time as a music venture was already coming to an end. 1970s' Dirty Stop Outs were the last generation to enjoy its musical offerings, including the bouncing balcony. It was a great venue, much loved and missed.

Rescued by Ziggy Stardust! Sue Long in her fave flares and platform boots. Inset above: Sue Long today

Queen appeared in November 1974 as part of their 'Sheer Heart Attack' tour. There probably were a few near heart attacks on that bouncing dress circle. They were supporting Mott the Hoople, who were more famous at that time though that was soon to be reversed.

When they returned the following November, their playlist included the unforgettable 'Bohemian Rhapsody' as well as 'Killer Queen'. They were becoming famous by then and no longer in the support role. Freddie Mercury was well on his way to becoming the global rock icon.

John Hewitt was there. "Queen were amazing and did 'Hey Big Spender' as an encore!" He also saw Ian Dury there in 1978.

Coventry Theatre did more than bring on the bands. They staged plays and musicals as well: it was a theatre after all.

Poster place and punk fan Miranda Aston

The Belgrade Theatre

Coventry's citizens were fortunate to live in a city of not just one but two theatres. Not far from the Coventry Theatre stood a newer one, the Belgrade, that offered much more than plays.

Opened in 1958, it was the first civic theatre to be built in the post-war period. Coventry's twin city - Belgrade in Serbia (formerly Yugoslavia) - pledged to give beech timber to be used in the new theatre and the ties between Coventry and Belgrade were sealed in the theatre's name.

Linda Kendall had her own special tie with the Belgrade: it had opened the same week that she was born.

"In April 1979 it was my 21st and also the Belgrade's. There was a special performance to which everyone born in the same week was given a pair of free tickets, so I took my mum."

Linda mentions the "free-flowing sparkling wine and birthday cake before the performance". They spotted Googie Withers, from the TV crime drama 'Within These Walls', among the guests as her daughter was one of the performers.

"I can't remember much about the show or who was performing, apart from Kenny Ball and his Jazzmen and Googie Withers's daughter, maybe because of all the pre-show refreshments!"

A memorable night for Linda even if the performance was largely forgotten!

This 21st celebration was a good example of the Belgrade connecting with Coventry citizens. Their offering was varied, not just 'high brow' plays.
The theatre promoted up and coming playwrights, community events and reached out to local schools with Theatre in Education.

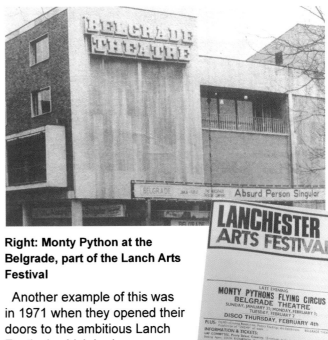

Right: Monty Python at the Belgrade, part of the Lanch Arts Festival

Another example of this was in 1971 when they opened their doors to the ambitious Lanch Festival, which had so many performances and acts going on they needed more venues.

When Monty Python's Flying Circus came to town it was the Belgrade where they performed. This was the first time the cast of the zany TV show had done a live stage performance. The theatre had to apply for special licences for three midnight shows. Even before these were approved, the Lanch festival office was 'swamped' with demand.

The shows were a big success as was the inter-venue co-operation that the Lanch festival had initiated which resulted in varied offerings at both of Coventry's theatres.

Status Quo play Coventry Theatre Photo: John Coles

Queen play Coventry Theatre Photo: John Coles

With the kind permission of the Cathedral Authorities

DARROL EDWARDS *presents*

A CONCERT *by*

Tangerine Dream

at

COVENTRY CATHEDRAL

Saturday, 4th October at 7.45 p.m.

Admission   - £1.35

No smoking in the Cathedral at any time
This ticket guarantees, but does not reserve a seat

COVENTRY Theatre
HALES STREET, COVENTRY

EVENING 7.30

12 SEP 1974

PROCUL HARUM STALLS   20P

STRIFE.

INCL. 10% VAT

A 16

Tickets sold cannot be
exchanged or taken back
TO BE RETAINED

COVENTRY Theatre
HALES STREET, COVENTRY

EVENING 7.30

Sunday, 16 Nov.

STALLS

QUEEN   £2.50
including V.A.T.

L 37

Tickets sold cannot be
exchanged or taken back
TO BE RETAINED

COVENTRY Theatre
HALES STREET, COVENTRY

EVENING 7.30

HAWKWIND

Thursday, 9 Dec.

STALLS
        £2.25
including V.A.T.

K 25

Tickets sold cannot be

COVENTRY Theatre
HALES STREET, COVENTRY

EVENING 7.30

SUPERTRAMP

Friday, 21 October

STALLS
        £3.00
including V.A.T.

GUEST

F18

Tickets sold cannot be
exchanged or taken back
TO BE RETAINED

COVENTRY Theatre
HALES ST., COVENTRY

EVENING 7.30

BLACK SABBATH.

Sunday, 9 June

STALLS
        £1.75
INCL. 10% VAT

N29

COVENTRY Theatre
HALES ST., COVENTRY

EVENING 7.30

10CC AND
Sunday, 15 Sept.

STALLS
        £1.20
including V.A.T.

E 6

Tickets sold cannot be
exchanged or taken back
TO BE RETAINED

COVENTRY Theatre
HALES ST., COVENTRY

EVENING 7.30

SPARKS + PILOT.

Sunday, 10 Nov.

STALLS
        £1.50
including V.A.T.

A16

Tick

COVENTRY Theatre
HALES STREET, COVENTRY

ALEX HARVEY

EVENING 7.30

Sunday, 2 May

STALLS
        £2.50
including V.A.T.

B 18

Tickets sold cannot be
exchanged or taken back
TO BE RETAINED

COVENTRY Theatre
HALES STREET, COVENTRY

EVENING 7.30

THIN LIZZY
Tuesday, 9 Nov.

STALLS
        £2.20
including V.A.T.

B15

Tickets sold cannot be
exchanged or taken back
TO BE RETAINED

WARWICK UNION

75p

Thur. Oct. 10

10CC AND UNICORN

Nº   456

COVENTRY Theatre
HALES STREET, COVENTRY

EVENING 7.30

Sunday, 16 Nov.

STALLS

QUEEN   £2.50
including V.A.T.

L 37

Tickets sold cannot be
exchanged or taken back
TO BE RETAINED

SOUNDS in association with **ROCK WORLD**
and **ATLANTIC RECORDS** presents

*'Lock Up Your
Daughters Tour'*

featuring **AC/DC**

at the CIVIC HALL, BEDWORTH

on THURSDAY, 17th JUNE, 1976

Tickets: £1.00   Nº   166

70s concert tickets, John Coles collection

FEEDING COVENTRY'S DIRTY STOP OUTS OF THE ERA

Colin Horton with partner Esther

'Hungry Mood? Enjoy our Food!'

It wasn't posh, didn't have a big menu and it certainly didn't look anything special. But the Specials, Coventry's 2-Tone pioneers were diehard fans of the Parson's Nose in Bishops Street – the small takeaway with a huge reputation. They were partial to the eatery's very own 'specials' which they immortalised in their 'Friday Night, Saturday Morning' single.

It was the must-go to destination for late-night revellers. Let's face it - marathon pub crawls and dancing are generally followed by big appetites and the need to 'soak up' some of the beer. Fried chicken joints and McDonalds were decades away so the Parson's Nose, ran by Louie and his family, was hard to pass by without ordering at least a faggot and pea batch.

A 'batch' (in case you were wondering) is a type of bread roll, just another of those Coventry things!

A 'rather large Greek lady' served up the food promptly and was often called 'mom.' But Maria didn't take any cheek from customers whose manners might have been adversely affected by alcohol. She was not to be

messed with. There was friendly banter in the queue about what they did or didn't get up to that night.

Not far away in The Burges was another cracking little café - Farmer Giles. People remember the very 'well rounded' gentleman there who buttered the bread and took the money. When he sat down for his own dinner, he could put away a very large plate full according to those who witnessed the sight.

> Colin Horton: **"I really loved going to the Parson's Nose after a night out for their famous "one- all in"- faggots, peas and chips on a take-out tray!"**

It was popular with football fans after a home game either celebrating or drowning their sorrows in chips. Many football fans walked through the city centre to and from Coventry City FC's Highfield Road ground. On the menu: Vienna steak, sausage or pastie with chips and the famous 'spesh'- steak and kidney pie, chips, peas and a cuppa plus bread and butter. Mouth-watering and all for just 2/6d!

Sherry Gorman's parents owned a few cafés in the city. They transformed a dress shop in Ironmonger Row into a Wimpy. Her dad Derek later incorporated it into his new Mr. Big chain and opened another in Trinity Street which then became a Wimpy Bar.

Trev Teasdel and friend Steve ('Scon') 'hung out' there in 1972, 'writing poems, lyrics and trying to change the world'.

Irene Bolger hadn't got time for writing poems as she was busy working there. "I made the ice cream and served. I didn't stay long after we had to pick the mouldy bits out of the batches and cut it off the cheese upstairs."

The iconic Round Cafe

Kim Hughes had a Saturday job at the Fairfax Street Wimpy Bar and sometimes had to work at the Trinity Street branch. "I also had to go to the 'circular cafe' as that was a Wimpy at that time. Waiting staff had to make their own dessert orders; knickerbocker glory's, brown Derby's, ice cream floats. I loved making them!'

Gill Dawson worked there for a while and wasn't particularly enamoured with the coffee. Her verdict? "Awful"!

The 'circular café' in the Lower Precinct was also known to many as the 'round café'. It was nice piece of post-war architecture and had various incarnations over the years. It was well placed to attract hungry or thirsty shoppers.

Local man John Starkey liked it and even wrote a poem about it:

They built a little café,
As round, as round could be.
A lovely place to have a snack,
A coffee or a tea.

They placed it on a pedestal,
So far above the ground,
And to this day some folk believe,
That it spun round and round.
(Extracts from The Round Café)

The Precinct looking towards the Round Cafe

For fish and chips, you couldn't beat Fishy Moores. It was one of Coventry's culinary landmarks and queues would form before they opened at lunchtime. Mr. Chignell ran the restaurant from 1957 till 1971 and his sister-in-law was married to the owner, Jack Moore. When it was sold in 1971 the new owners moved it to Fairfax Street, opposite the bus station and near to Coventry's Olympic sized swimming pool. A bag of chips after a swim was a must!

For Linda Kendall and her mum, a visit into town sometimes included a nice picnic in Lady Herbert's Garden with chips bought from Fishy Moores.

Coventry Corporation still had some of its own eateries for citizens. Basic canteens for those bombed out of their homes had been replaced by the likes of licensed restaurant The Mercia Grill which opened in July 1971. It had self-service and waitress service with each section named after local areas such as the Warwick Room. The Mercia became a nightclub in 1978.

The Bridge Restaurant in Broadgate was another example of efforts to feed Coventry citizens in style.

Another place offering good food with a pleasant ambience was the Captain's Table. It was similar to the Cottage in the Burges which later became The Chaumiére.

Maureen Bucknall: **"You could get a good meal in the Bridge Restaurant, it was about the only place really in the early '70s. I would sometimes go there with my husband John."**

View of Bridge Restaurant, Broadgate

Singer Sue Starr and first husband Mick eating Medieval style

Going for a Medieval

Though Coventry was a modern city, the '70s saw a fad for going right back in time for dinner. It could get messy, but historic Coombe Abbey on the outskirts of the city, offered the full-on medieval feast experience.

Dating back to the 13th century, the abbey had gone through various reincarnations. In 1971 the buildings were leased to Historic Productions Ltd who hosted grand medieval banquets. Stories of

monks and servants whose ghosts haunted the place didn't put people off!

Local singer Sue Starr was one of many who enjoyed a night out there with colleagues from the Jaguar works. Guests entering the banqueting hall were greeted and seated at wooden tables and benches by hooded monks.

Sue Lowe went to a 'Christmas special' there. The ladies of the court, dressed in medieval costumes, sang carols, including the 'Coventry

Joe and Babs Lee, left, enjoying a Medieval Banquet with friends

> Sue Starr: "We were given mead to drink and had bibs tied round our necks then ate our meal with our fingers, great fun! We had to pick a couple to be crowned king and queen for the evening. We were also entertained by the court jester and the ladies of the court sang to us."

Carol'. The court jester helped everyone get into the spirit of things.

She remembers it as being "soup to start, served in wooden bowls and eaten with wooden spoons, chicken and jacket potato for main – no implements at all. And apple crumble for pudding, again, in a wooden bowl with wooden spoons, all washed down with rustic cups of mead and red wine in goblets."

Each course, called "a remove'" as in "the first remove, broth," was announced as it was served. Sue remembers the chicken being cooked with lots of herbs and the apple crumble flavoured with cinnamon, served with custard or cream which was all "really delicious".

Going for an Indian, Chinese or a continental

In the 1970s people were getting more adventurous in their eating habits, partly due to holidays abroad, changing food production and marketing techniques.

> Sue Lowe: "Once a week I ate fried fish and salad for my tea at the Swiss Alps next to the Smithfield Hotel. It was delicious. I used to go there between working in Massey-Ferguson's office during the day and my evening class, around 1978."

The Swiss Alps restaurant, opened in 1971, had a continental feel and appeal. The themed restaurant was the brainchild of adventurous Croatian entrepreneur Ivan Polancec. He and his Spanish wife imported Swiss costumes, dirndl dresses and snow-white blouses, for the waitresses and put skis on the wall. There was also a large mural of a snowy mountain on one wall.

Ivan didn't restrict his imagination to his restaurants - he turned his suburban home into something resembling a film set for Julius Caesar. He certainly liked to be different!

Stuart Beamish would "stop by at the Alps" after the Saturday home match for omelette and chips. This was "to ready the stomach for what was to come on Saturday night!"

A new Italian restaurant, Roma Nello, opened in the City Arcade

in 1973 and immediately caught everyone's attention. The owner, Nello Minelli, had settled in Coventry in the late '50s and his restaurant was a great addition to the city's nightlife. There were dinner and dances - very popular in the '70s - for New Year's Eve and other special occasions.

Nello's became a popular drinking venue after time was called in the pubs because of its late licence. Other restaurants served this role as a place to legally have one or two for the road.

Colin Horton sometimes finished up there in the wee hours of Monday morning. "After half price drinks at George's till 12, we would head to Nello's for chicken in the basket and more beer till 2am." What about work? No problem. Like thousands of car workers across the city, Colin was on the night shift so could sleep in the daytime.

The Golden Orient One was one of the first Chinese restaurants in Coventry. Ted Duggan was amazed by the menu and went every week to try a different dish. "It was the first time I ever tried boiled rice and curry and lemon tea."

No prizes for guessing that the Pagoda - set in the Precinct's Hillman House - was a Chinese restaurant. Sue Lowe and her husband were customers there. "It was in a block of flats next to Allied Carpets. I can still recall the taste of lychees, and attempting to use

chopsticks. I also remember the Great Wall restaurant which was up a steep flight of stairs in the City Arcade."

The New Orient on Hales Street was also popular with three-course business lunches for the bargain price of 50p and luncheon vouchers could be used for this midday feast.

Joe Reynolds remembers it had a limited menu but was cheap with an added attraction: "Most of us

> Tony Unwin: **"Nello's was a respectable restaurant by day which evolved into a small night club/drinking den by night. Men usually wouldn't get in without a tie."**

fancied the Chinese girl who served the sweet and sour pork. She was lovely and probably knew that we all fancied her. She had a nice personality."

Meryl Barrett recalls another bit of fancying going on there. Must have been something in the chop suey! "My friend and I were always in the New Orient, even when we should have been at school. We would buy a tea and stay for ages. My friend fancied one of the guys who worked there because she thought he looked like Bruce Lee!"

Trev Teasdel fancied the Chinese pancakes. "I thought I'd try one, only to find it was full of bean sprouts, not what I was expecting. 'Mouldy Old Dough' had just come out and someone coincidentally put it on the jukebox. It seemed to express my disappointment. I'd never had bean sprouts up until then!"

Going for an Indian often meant the Rajah in Cross Cheaping where Sue Lowe had her first taste of curry. "Chicken dahnsak with chips, in 1976. Deliciously spicy

with an abundance of flock wallpaper and jangly music playing in the background."

Just Hanging Around!

The café on the top floor of Woolies was very popular and it wasn't just shoppers tucking into fish and chips. Young people found it was a good spot to hang around - especially on Saturdays.

Colin Horton and his mates would also hang around after the Locarno. "We would go to the bowling alley above the car park then to Woolies café."

The Kongoni was a small coffee house tucked away down an alley off the Precinct. Trev Teasdel loved its ambience. "The smoky cafe, the table at the back, in the corner, 1972,1973, bohemian Coventry poets, long hair, beards, ashtrays, smoke rings, fag packets, rollups and matches."

"There was rebellion in the air",' says Trev, "as well as lots of smoke

> Meryl Barrett: **"After the Locarno on Saturday mornings, it was down to Woolies café where we'd never buy anything but stand along the balcony and stairwell and socialise plus eye up the boys!"**

They drank just enough coffee to be allowed to stay. The quality of the coffee was superb. The large machine at the back of the shop behind the sacks of coffee was a roaster, not a grinder. The grinding was all done at the counter at the time of sale.

Meryl Barrett loved walking past the Kongoni with that wonderful smell of the coffee. But she had to keep walking as she can't drink coffee. For Valerie Haudiquet, the coffee smell got mixed up with that from the nearby Canadian Furs Shop. "When I was really tiny, I knew nothing about the Kongoni so I thought fur coats smelt of coffee!"

> Trev Teasdel: **"The seductive smell of Kenyan coffee hit the nostrils before you entered the Kongoni."**

For the Rhythm Doctor "there was only one really, Noel's café on the side street next to the General Wolfe". It was very handy for those needing food and a cup of something before or after gigs held at the pub. Noel's was frequented by local band members as well and later was the setting for a video of 'Jungle Music', by Special AKA featuring Rico, in 1982.

Whatever their tastes, 1970s Coventry's Dirty Stop Outs didn't go hungry with plenty of places to choose from and plenty of different cuisines, menus and atmospheres.

Mr and Mrs Metcalfe drink to retirement.

DUNCAN and Joyce Metcalfe are looking for a permanent coffee break.

The couple, both 67, are hoping to retire — if they can find a buyer for the Kongoni Coffe Company which they opened in Coventry City centre 21 years ago.

The leasehold premises in Market Way are up for sale for £85,000.

Since Mr and Mrs Metcalf of Asthill Grove, Coventry, started their business they have increased their turnover in fresh coffee sales twenty fold.

They choose their own beans from a London merchant and roast and blend them on the premises. Mrs Metcalfe also runs a small cafeteria upstairs.

"We can do the mental work standing on our heads," said Mrs Metcalfe. "But lifting 150lb sacks of coffee beans and being on your feet 10 hours a day is too difficult for us now."

The couple's chief concern is to find the right buyer.

"We'd like to make sure the business continues exactly as it is," said Mr Metcalfe. "And we're quite prepared to stay on for a while and break the new person in."

Mr Metcalfe became a coffee taster with Twinings in London in 1931, took a job in the coffee business in Kenya in 1936 and, apart from the war years, has never worked with anything else.

"We had planned to start our own coffee farm in Kenya, but when the country became independent we decided to come home instead," recalled Mr Metcalfe. "We had to stick to what we knew, and all I knew was coffee."

They were walking along Fleet Street in London and noticed the "Coventry Evening Telegraph" office. They advertised in the paper and were offered the lease on their present site.

BANDS AND VENUES GALORE

CHAPTER 8

John Hewitt's drumming career began early!

NEW WAVE MUSIC FROM: Blown Fuze SAT 22nd SEPT at the Queen INN (off Sidney Stringer schol) - Primrose Hill St DOORS OPEN: 8.00 ADMISSION [40P] 38

There were so many bands forming, splitting up and regrouping in 1970s Coventry it was hard to keep up. And there could never be too many venues on the circuit for them to play at way back then.

Playing in a band or three...

John Hewitt's career was typical of many other musicians in the '70s. His ambition to play drums started early - he had a cardboard drum kit plus friends in his 'band' aged about 12! But things quickly moved up a gear.

"I played in local band Solid Grease in 1976, which became The Fuze, then by 1979 Blown Fuze." In 1978 John was also in punk covers bands the Pseuds and Dealer. "The Pseuds only did a few gigs in Coventry. In 1978 I played at Dog and Trumpet in Dealer. It was underground and hot but not a bad stage and good acoustics."

> Trev Teasdel: **"It's funny, there was always a feeling that Coventry was a 'cultural desert,' a feeling of "nothin' ever 'appens" but looking at all the venues and bands, we were so lucky!"**

There were other gigs in Dealer and Blown Fuze at the Antelope Motor Cycle club. He remembers it being a '"biker's place, with the stage upstairs". This later became Careys. John also played at the City Centre Club in his various bands.

His funniest memory of 1979 was of a Blown Fuze rehearsal at a school in Keresley. "I put a poster on the toilet /cupboard door. The cleaner refused to clean it as she thought the fuses were really blown... and I spelt it with a Z as well!"

How did they choose the quirky band names? They did what David Bowie did: wrote words on bits of paper, mixed them up, pulled some out and saw what came up.

The 'circuit' for bands that John Hewitt played in included the Zodiac pub near the Parsons Nose and

**Mark Byers
of Wild Boys**
Photo: Rob
Lapworth

the Swanswell Tavern, which later became the White Swan. John helped to get Queens Inn on the circuit after asking if they would let them use the function room. They agreed so John and his band started using it and others followed. They had to carry the gear from one pub to another if no transport was available.

At one gig he hit the cymbal so hard the stand fell over causing irreparable damage. "That meant the door money was gone! We had to replace the cymbal!"

Like many band members, John had a day job. He worked at the Coventry Climax and at the start of 1979 he struck up a friendship there with another musician, Mick Galic: "Mick noticed I was wearing a Ludwig drum badge and we started chatting about bands. He then joined ours!" Two years on Mick was in Dexy's Midnight Runners, playing on their big hit Come on Eileen in 1982.

John was "pretty amazed" to later find himself in one of Coventry's most successful bands of the '80s - King. "People at work used to laugh at me and Mick, only a few thought we'd do well!" They proved the doubters wrong.

Another popular band on the circuit was the Wild Boys. Formed by Roddy 'Radiation' Byers in the mid-70s, he later left to join the Specials. Keeping it in the family, his younger

brother Mark, along with Johnnie Thomson and Rob Lapworth, took over. With 15-years-old Tony Lynch on drums, they rehearsed at Johnnie's mother's small, terraced house in Kerseley village. The volume had to be kept right down and Tony had to be satisfied hitting his drumsticks on a stool!

They did their first gig as The Extras in the garden of nearby pub - the Golden Eagle - playing mainly Bowie, Iggy and Bolan covers. It was described as "a slightly ramshackle event". Their first proper gig in front of a likeminded audience was in the downstairs bar at the Lanch with local bands Squad and Urge.

The band reverted to the name Wild Boys as they began to get regular gigs and headlined at a Fresher's Ball at the Lanch.

Popular punk band Squad was originally fronted by Terry Hall but he moved to the Automatics, later to become the Specials, after being spotted by Jerry Dammers.

John Hewitt on drums

With Gus Chambers taking his place, they brought out the single 'Red Alert' in 1978 with 'Eight pound a Week' on the flip side. This got them noticed. Then in 1979 their 'Millionaire/Brockhill Boys' was released.

Miranda Aston: "Every night you could see a punk or a reggae band".

Pete Chambers wrote that Gus had "punk crazed stage antics but he fronted the band through their finest moments". He also judged them as "without a doubt they were the finest punk band that ever came from this beloved city of ours".

Coventry bands had a wide circuit to cover if they had the energy. And if their day jobs didn't get in the way of course.

More venues

Most large factories set up clubs for their employees, some being very impressive. At Matrix Machine Tools, the works canteen was transformed into a dance hall at weekends. Supertramp played at the Matrix before they became famous, as well as Cockney Rebel. The Wild Boys also gigged there.

Christine Venning: "We saw a lot of top stars at the Matrix out on the Highway. So many of the workplaces had sports and social clubs, so there was a lot going on!"

Coventry's many social clubs provided important practice and gig spaces for bands of all kinds. They provided regular work for the city's musicians as well as a tough training ground.

In 1977 Ray Barrie joined a Coventry band named after a London underground line - Bakerloo. They was already well-established when he started playing bass with them, being popular on the social club circuit as well as at private events: "They played a mix of well-known popular songs as well as current chart favourites".

Liz Smith: "There used to be great live bands at Stoke Ex-Services on Saturday nights which was our club. My ex-husband played in a group called Something Good and gigged in a lot of the CIU clubs."

They were under no illusion about the main attraction when playing in the clubs - bingo! "I remember many times when most people would leave a club after the final bingo session of the night. We would then go on stage to a much-reduced audience. But it was regular work and paid better than the few pubs still holding live music events."

Ray had been in other bands including Memories who "played hits and were suitable for all ages and tastes". They also had a residency at the Smithfield Arms, across the road from the Coventry Theatre.

Wild Boys rehearsing

Wild Boys Poster and Wild Boys play at the Matrix Hall Photos: Rob Lapworth

Tony Unwin was at the Royal Naval Club sometime in 1973, looking forward to Vinegar Joe, featuring Elkie Brooks. "Me and my mates had coughed up 50 pence for tickets, a lot of money in those days!" But the band didn't show as Ms Brooks was ill.

At THE WALSGRAVE
A BLUES CONCERT
Tuesday, September 1st, 1970
★ LAST FAIR DEAL ★
★ GYPSY LEE ★
★ ROD FELTON (Electric) ★
TICKETS 3/-

"We were offered our money back or a half refund and replacement band. As we were looking forward to seeing a live band, we went for the latter option."

Disappointment followed. "The band from Birmingham

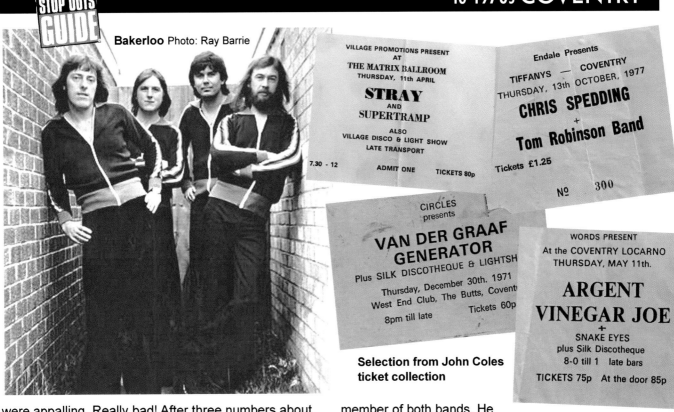

Bakerloo Photo: Ray Barrie

VILLAGE PROMOTIONS PRESENT
AT
THE MATRIX BALLROOM
THURSDAY, 11th APRIL

STRAY
AND
SUPERTRAMP

ALSO
VILLAGE DISCO & LIGHT SHOW
LATE TRANSPORT

7.30 - 12   ADMIT ONE   TICKETS 80p

Endale Presents
TIFFANYS — COVENTRY
THURSDAY, 13th OCTOBER, 1977

CHRIS SPEDDING
+
Tom Robinson Band

Tickets £1.25

Nº 300

CIRCLES
presents

VAN DER GRAAF GENERATOR
Plus SILK DISCOTHEQUE & LIGHTSH
Thursday, December 30th, 1971
West End Club, The Butts, Covent
8pm till late   Tickets 60p

WORDS PRESENT
At the COVENTRY LOCARNO
THURSDAY, MAY 11th.

ARGENT
VINEGAR JOE
+
SNAKE EYES
plus Silk Discotheque
8-0 till 1   late bars

TICKETS 75p   At the door 85p

Selection from John Coles ticket collection

were appalling. Really bad! After three numbers about ten of us adjourned to the nearest pub in disgust. The band? Judas Priest! They made it on an enormous scale a few years later."

Paris was another local band in the late '70s that performed in clubs and other venues. It emerged out of Drops of Brandy, a well known, semi-professional covers band according to Tim Constable who was a

member of both bands. He described the style of music played by Paris as 'high energy prog pop!'

They developed some of their own material and did some recordings as well. The late '70s saw the rise of 2-Tone and bands that didn't offer that type of sound found it increasingly harder to get bookings and professional recognition. They folded in 1982.

Miranda Aston and friends at a gig on Hearsall Common

A bit of jazz and folk

Nº 407

HENLEY COLLEGE FOLK CLUB

presents

THE YETTIES

Plus Residents

FOLKLORE

on WEDNESDAY, SEPTEMBER, 27th, 1972

at the NEW INN, LONGFORD ROAD

Starts 8.00   Price 35p

COMPLEMENTARY

THE GATE FOLK CLUB

FOR FOLK WITH SOUL

SUNDAY NIGHT 8:00 PM

YWCA. THE BUTTS, COVENTRY.

Old Dyers Arms

Jack Ashby reminds us that wartime dance bands were still popular well into the 1970s with both modern and traditional jazz firmly established in the city. Key venues included the GEC Ballroom as well as the Mercers Arms, Earlsdon Cottage and Weavers Arms. The Leofric Hotel was another destination for jazz fans.

Ray Barrie thinks there should be a plaque for where the Mercers Arms stood. "Many top acts came up from London to perform there over the years including Rod Stewart. I played there in several bands in the '70s and '80s, as did many other Coventry bands."

Valerie Haudiquet recalls a jazz band at the Cottage with "an average age of 95! They were excellent".

A longstanding folk music scene was also thriving in 1970s. Musicians such as Ben Arnold, local folk club organiser and pioneer, had done much to lay the foundations in the 1960s for the next generation to continue.

All types of folk music was on offer with those learning the art appearing in small, smoke-filled pubs. Singer Pauline Black of Selecter enjoyed folk and sang in places like the Old Dyers Arms in the Butts.

Other folk haunts included the Bear Inn's Rocky Road club and the Lanch Poly Folk Club. The latter held in the infamous downstairs bar with its plastic glasses on desk type tables surrounded by murals from the '60s of scenes from Tolkien's Lord of the Rings. Local performers were welcome and well-known singers turned up such as Rod Felton. Thursday nights at the Colin Campbell were usually given over to the folk club and many local musicians also played there over the years.

Coventry folk musician Ben Arnold

Ben Arnold at his day job

COVENTRY'S 2-TONE REVOLUTION

CHAPTER 9

As the decade neared its end something very special was happening - the emergence of a sound that would define the city like never before. People were increasingly tuning in to Coventry's new musical style - an incendiary mix of of punk, ska, reggae and rocksteady .

This was 2-Tone - an inspirational movement that would quickly become a worldwide cultural phenomenon. Over four decades on, people are still talking about it, listening and dancing to it.

Pete Chambers quickly saw that 2-Tone was vibrant, hard hitting and shaking things up. It would certainly shake up his own life!

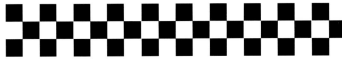

"1979 was the year it all changed for Coventry as 2-Tone Records put the city on the music map. It was multicultural, it was style, it was dance. We're very proud of its enduring existence."

Long-term 2-Tone fan Nick Edgington said: "Even now there are 2-Tone and ska Facebook groups and at least one bar I know of in Benidorm, that wouldn't exist without the Specials."

The rapid rise of 2-Tone coincided with the equally rapid decline of Coventry's main industry. The city had seen its first car produced - a Daimler - way back in 1897. The local economy had grown to become heavily reliant on the car factories.

2-Tone, for many young people, provided a sense of excitement and optimism despite the catatrophic demise of the city's industrial base together with thousands of jobs.

1979 brought another new arrival. Mrs Thatcher swept into power on May 4th as the country's first female Prime Minister. Her authoritarian - and for many divisive - style of politics was something else you couldn't ignore and she was soon firmly in the crosshairs of much of the nation's disenfranchised youth. Her arrival fuelled interest in the movement even more.

What made 2-Tone so special? It can be loosely described as a mix of reggae, ska, rocksteady and punk. The latter had already been big in Coventry. Miranda Aston saw punk as a step change in many ways. 2-Tone picked up on all of that, added the creativity of local musicians plus a chunk of Coventry attitude to bring it all together. It also needed their cheek, charisma and their chomping at the bit to break some rules.

Young Rude Boy Pete Chambers

2-Tone musicians had seen previous generations twisting, rocking and pogo-ing the night away. They had their own ideas about a ska revival with some punk mixed in, whilst paying due respect to the West Indian and reggae roots. They didn't dismiss their musical predecessors - they acknowledged their achievements and wanted to take them to another level.

2-Tone was musical fusion at its best: entertaining, great to dance to and, at the heart, lyrics that meant something to young people. The mixing of cultures, with black and white musicians in the line-ups, was a highly visible statement that went way beyond pop music.

Multiculturalism was at the core and the desire to overcome the racial tensions of the time. 2-Tone emerged as Rock against Racism was getting going so there were close links, as there had been with punk. And it came with its own defining fashion style - black and white check.

How did it come about?

Before 2-Tone Coventry was ska and reggae central in many ways with the local Afro-Caribbean community contributing a great deal to the city's music and dance scene. Many white kids, seeing something different, were happy to join in the fun.

Charley Anderson of the Selecter getting lively

Federal International Organisation, Coventry
present

The 11th Jamaica Independence Dance

Ladies and Gentlemen, A Great Night awaits you

on FRIDAY, 9th AUGUST, 1974
at St. Osburgs Hall, Upper Hill Street, Coventry

WHEN WE PRESENT TO YOU, THE ONE AND ONLY

Desmond Deck

A key venue was, bizarrely, the police ballroom in Little Park Street. Refurbished with a modern sprung dance floor, it was used not just for official police and civic events but as a function room for hire.

Coventry pop star Don Fardon and the Soul Machine played there, as did Jimmy James and the Vagabonds. Coventry's Association of Overseas Students used it for gigs and, lacking their own social centre, local West Indian organisers used it as well.

> Neol Davies: **"Ray King made me aware that you could do something other on the stage than play, you could also entertain."**

Growing in popularity, the police ballroom attracted big names such as Desmond Dekker who also topped the bill for the 11th Jamaican Independence dance in 1974 at St. Osburg's Hall.

Ray King and his Soul Band played at the police ballroom. A charismatic and popular showman, he became an important role model for aspiring local musicians, as well as an inspiration for 2-Tone bands. He encouraged the sharing of music and cultures and promoted racial harmony. Ray acted as mentor to younger musicians such as Neol Davies and Charley Anderson of The Selecter.

The Ray King Soul Band gigged regularly across Coventry including at the Mercer's Arms, the Railway Club as well as the Locarno. Local fame led to national then international bookings and Ray opened up a new musical route for younger musicians.

An important place for young talent was the Holyhead Road Youth Centre with its concert hall. It had stage on the ground floor and a music workshop. Youth worker Charley Anderson rehearsed reggae style with young musicians, some later forming and joining 2-Tone bands.

Young 2-Tone fan Lee O'Hara proudly showing off his black and white gear

When Coventry-based arts group and magazine Hobo moved there in 1974, a creative coming together was bound to happen. This took place in July when Neol Davies, jamming upstairs, popped downstairs and ended up playing with Charley and the others.

Their sessions became fairly regular after that. Charley worked with Ray King to set up creative activities around music and they were instrumental in helping to get the centre refurbished, again aiding the emergence of 2-Tone. Many collaborations started up and bands formed, then reformed.

> Nick Edgington: **"We were suddenly in the national spotlight. It was a good feeling that Coventry's music was now cool. The NME did an article on the Cov scene and I was proud about having seen all the bands they mentioned. Lots of talent scouts came looking for the new sensation and lot of singles from bands I'd seen locally came out: I still have them!'**

Holyhead Road Youth Centre

Inset: Analog at a Hobo workshop, at the Centre

Coming together - the Specials

Members of the Specials were already dotted around Coventry and having an impact years before they came together as the band that shot to worldwide fame .

Jerry Dammers attended local boys school, King Henry VIIIth, then the Lanch Poly. He was a founding member of the band in 1977, played keyboards and wrote songs. Jamaican-born Neville Staple lived in Coventry and worked with sound systems before joining the band. He worked with DJ Pete Waterman at the Locarno who soon saw the potential of the style of music.

Horace Panter had come to Coventry to study fine art and joined as bassist along with guitarist Roddy 'Radiation' Byers, formerly of the Wild Boys. Jamaican born Lynval Golding moved to Coventry when he was 18. He was vocals and rhythm guitar. Terry Hall left Squad and replaced Tim Strickland as vocalist. John Bradbury (Brad) had been playing drums in Coventry for years when Trev Teasdel first heard him in 1970 when they collaborated on some songs.

> Nick Edgington: **"It was great to rub shoulders with blokes you'd seen on Top of the Pops. I stood next to the Special's Roddy Radiation in the General Wolfe's gents one night and didn't mind that he splashed my Docs!"**

> Lizzi Maxted: **"When I worked as a barmaid at the Albany pub, they used to come in for a pint or two after rehearsals across the road."**

"Brad was a great drummer even then back in 1970. No fancy stuff, just very skilful. He joined in an all-night jam session at the Umbrella organised by Al Docker and involved Neol Davies as lead musician. It was the first time Neol and Brad played together and later they did the track that became the B side of 'Gangsters'."

The band were originally called the Automatics. The Rhythm Doctor remembers the excitement of being at their first gig at the Heath Hotel. They played pubs across the city including their local, the Albany, in

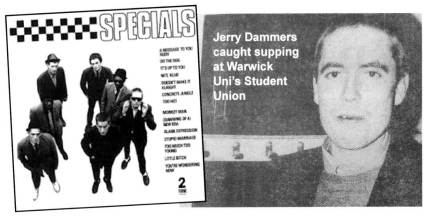

Jerry Dammers caught supping at Warwick Uni's Student Union

Earlsdon which was close to the 'epicentre' of 2-Tone - 51 Albany Road.

Over in Far Gosford Street, the Hand and Heart pub had earlier hosted the Coventry punk scene before accommodating the emerging 2-Tone musicians.

The Selecter played there as did the Automatics. Steve 'Cardboard' Eaton was the original DJ there and what he did with ska music became legendary. His was the face on the cover of The Selecter album, 'Too Much Pressure'.

Pete Chambers talks of the excited anticipation when the band went on stage. "As the infectious ska rhythms began, they teased us all, defying us not to dance, when we all knew it was virtually impossible."

The Selecter's Pauline Black became a role model for many aspiring female singers. She was out there in front, confident, cool and chic, often delivering strong messages in the lyrics.

It was history in the making and a great time to be right at the heart of it, in Coventry.

When the Specials played at Warwick University's Anti-Nazi League concert in 1979, they were described as a "new wave/ reggae band". They were joined by Terry Hall's previous band Squad and God's Toys. There was a bit of bother as some of the audience surged forward. Things got lively but no real trouble broke out.

As the rest of the country took note, the London-based music press did too. They had no choice but to venture into the 'Badlands of the industrial West Midlands,' as Pete Chambers put it, probably put out that this movement wasn't London-based. "What had wrongly been considered a quaint musical backwater was now in focus and Coventry kids were proud".

```
                                        26/9/73.

Dear Trev,
           would be much obliged if you could include this
in the classified section of your mag.

           BASSIST, (student, 50watt gear, limited experience)
           Seeks happy band.
      Write, Horace, Top flat,
           12 Binley Road,
           Coventry.
I reckon that puts it into the 10p. bracket, so please find
same somewhere in the envelope.
                     Best of luck with the mag,
                                        Horace.
```

Horace Panter seeking a 'happy band' to play in

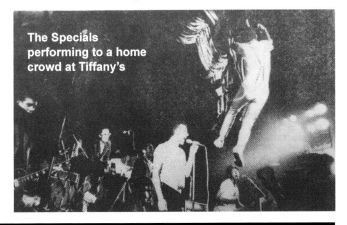

The Specials performing to a home crowd at Tiffany's

The Specials first single, 'Gangsters', was released on their own 2-Tone record label based at Jerry Dammers' house in Albany Road. Valerie Haudiquet was living at the Albany Road HQ. "I remember when Jerry bought the first batch home. My little old mum and dad were there. Jerry put it on our Dansette and dad told us it was very 'toe tappy'. I had piles of copies!"

> Pete Chambers: **"The record buying public took to the first 2-Tone record in their masses. 'Gangsters' Vs 'The Selecter', show-cased this tantalising cross-fade of ska and punk perfectly. Ten thousand Dansettes dropped the fancy labelled disc onto the turntable, to the delight of the boys and girls of rudeness."**

Nick Edgington saw Special AKA at the Butts Technical College's Student Union. "Three bands for 80p! I bought their 'Gangsters' single there, hand stamped by Jerry Dammers." The single was also a bargain. "I think it was 50p. I remember Terry Hall saying, in his normal sarcastic tone, 'This our new single. Go out and buy it and make it number one!' So, I did, and it was!"

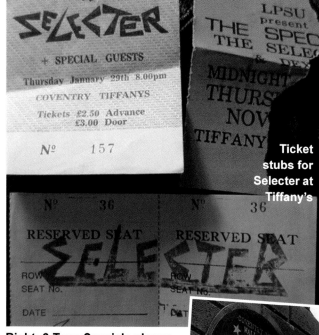

Ticket stubs for Selecter at Tiffany's

Val Haudiquet catching up with Jerry Dammers, Spatial AKA Orchestra concert, 2012

Right: 2-Tone Specials plaque in Coventry's 2-Tone Village

It wasn't to everyone's taste though. After one recording session at Coventry's Horizon studio, one of the engineers played 'Gangsters' by the Specials for Ray Barrie. "I said I didn't like it. The rest is history."

Right: Nick Edgington's prized Special AKA vs Gangster single

Remembering Terry Hall

December 18th, 2022 brought the sad news that Terry Hall had passed away, aged 63. This hit hard in Coventry, his home city, where he was well-known and liked. There was a sense of shock, even disbelief that he'd gone.

Over the course of his almost 50-year career he had sang and talked about the city's upsides and downsides, the good times and the bad. Terry sang and spoke for a generation of Coventry's youth.

Nick Edgington describes it in this way. "He was a big part of my life in the late '70s and early '80s, with both the Specials and the Fun Boy Three. They put Coventry on the musical map, even singing about it and places we all knew. There was a real buzz about the city for a few years."

Pete Chambers talks of how you would never know what was going to transpire at a Specials gig, and

"what words of sardonic wit Mr Terry Hall would deliver". Terry Hall stood out and had an impact on audiences.

Many obituaries have recounted Terry's musical career with local bands – Squad, Automatics, Specials, then later with Fun Boy Three, The Colourfield plus many other collaborations. He was still working before he died, still so much music left in him and plans to fulfil. They were not to be.

For many, he'll always be that young Specials frontman, singing those unforgettable lines: "You've done too much, much too young". He's left us thinking "Terry, you've gone too soon, much too young."

2-Tone plaque for the Hand and Heart pub

HITS AND NEAR MISSES

1	1	MOULDY OLD DOUGH LIEUTENANT PIGEON	£	DECCA F 13278
2	10	DONNA 10c.c.		UK 6
3	3	YOU'RE A LADY PETER SKELLERN	£	DECCA F 13333
4	2	HOW CAN I BE SURE DAVID CASSIDY	○	BELL BELL 1298
5	4	I DIDN'T KNOW I LOVED YOU (Till I Saw You Rock 'N' Roll) bell GARY GLITTER		BELL 1250
6	5	IN A BROKEN DREAM PYTHON LEE JACKSON	£	YOUNGBLOOD YB 1002
7	6	BURNING LOVE ELVIS PRESLEY	£	RCA 2267
8	8	WIG WAM BAM SWEET		RCA 2260
9	17	ELECTED ALICE COOPER	○	WARNER BROTHERS K 16214
10	5	CHILDREN OF THE REVOLUTION T REX	○	EMI MARC 2
11	11	BIG SIX JUDGE DREAD		BIG SHOT BI 608

OCT. 21

COMPUTER chart played by the BBC and compiled for Record & Tape Retailer/Record Mirror, 7 Carnaby Street, London, by British Market Research Bureau.

☝ FORECAST

○ ¼ MILLION SALES

○ MILLION SALES

£ SALES INCREASING

Top
of the
charts!
Mouldy
Old
Dough

Lieutenant Pigeon early 70s-Nigel, Steve, Rob and Rob's mum Hilda

In 1972 Coventry band Lieutenant Pigeon was suddenly launched into the spotlight with their quirky, surprise hit 'Mouldy Old Dough' which also earned them a place in the music hall of fame.

It might have had something to do with front man Rob Woodward's endearing mum, Hilda - she turned up on piano. It can only have been helped by the fact it was released in the early '70s - a period that was a bit all over the place music-wise anyway.

It was a definite thumbs down from The Guardian: "Only in 1972 could a track this ramshackle and mildewed have got to No 1. It's a jaunty tune hammered into dementia on the piano, accompanied by troglodyte drums and a tatterdemalion pipe – and, of course, Nigel Fletcher's unspeakable vocals..."

The Belgians were fond of it and after airtime on Radio Luxemburg it hit the top spot here. It sold over two million copies worldwide and the 'Pigeons received that year's Ivor Novello song-writing award.

Who'd have thought that a record featuring a young man and his 60- year-old mum would be so popular? This was a first mother-son pop partnership at the time

Young Hilda

Sue Starr: "We worked in her front room, I sang while she played the piano. She transposed sheet music for me into a key that was in my vocal range and we'd go through it again. She was a very pleasant lady who always wanted to make sure that you were happy with her work."

Local singer Susan Starr

and when Hilda appeared on Top of the Pops - well, that was another first for the band. They also used Hilda's living room to practice and record demo tapes.

Other band members included drummer Nigel Fletcher and Steve Johnson. Lieutenant Pigeon was preceded by Stavely Makepeace with Radio One DJs raving about their 1970 single 'Edna'. Annie Nightingale thought "it was the best thing since sliced tomatoes" and Noel Edmonds was "quite struck" by it.

The Pigeon's fame brought teeny bopper adoration. Nigel Fletcher and Rob Woodward remember one gig at the Locarno very clearly. "We were riding high in the music charts and did a matinee appearance to an audience of screaming 12 to 15-year olds!" They recognised one of them from their street and said that she wouldn't have given them the time of day before their hit.

Hilda was an accomplished pianist who, in her early years, played at Coventry's old picture houses and worked with local musicians and performers.

Hilda made many appearances but was talked out of going on the road. When she died in 1999, aged 85, she left behind a musical and family legacy.

Right: One Fine Day by Shel Naylor aka Rob Woodward

Hilda's Top of the Pops publicity pic

Lieutenant Pigeon flying high!

LIEUTENANT PIGEON

Another piece in the '70s Jigsaw

Another globally successful Coventry band was Jigsaw, best known for their aptly named hit single 'Sky High'. This was the theme tune for the film 'Man from Hong Kong' in 1976, starring George Lazenby.

Formed ten years earlier, the original band members from Coventry and nearby Rugby included singer-song writer duo Clive Scott and Des Dyer and guitarist /vocalist Tony Campbell. They began locally, honing their skills both as musicians and crowd pleasers. They were regulars at pubs and social clubs such as the Cheylesmore, Baginton Oak, the Parkstone and the Standard on Tile Hill Lane.

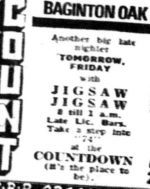

Jigsaw's hit single, Sky High

Right: Jigsaw at the Bagington Oak

Jigsaw in action

Their sheer hard work doing the rounds of local venues and holding down day jobs paid off after turning professional. They went on to produce more marketable pop music by the mid-1970s. They legacy includes an impressive catalogue of singles and albums with varying degrees of success.

> Annette Williscroft: **"Jigsaw were very popular and well liked. A very friendly band. I enjoyed seeing them play at the Walsgrave pub several times."**

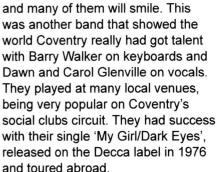

Jigsaw on TV

Their stage acts were something to remember with explosions, smashing or burning of drum kits and fire eating. Before 'Sky High', they won acclaim for the 1974 hit single 'Who Do You Think You Are?' This was later recorded by Candlewick Green who won the popular '70s TV talent show 'Opportunity Knocks'.

Local musician Donald Arthur Maughn found international fame as Don Fardon. He worked as a draughtsman at Alfred Herberts before becoming successful first with 'Indian Reservation' then with his 1970 hit 'Belfast Boy' that paid homage to football player George Best. His next hit was 'Follow your Drum', released in 1972.

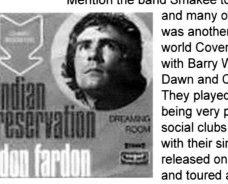

After 'Delta Queen' in 1973, his star faded. He went into the licensing trade and continued to entertain local people by running pubs in the Coventry area.

Mention the band Smakee to people of a certain age and many of them will smile. This was another band that showed the world Coventry really had got talent with Barry Walker on keyboards and Dawn and Carol Glenville on vocals. They played at many local venues, being very popular on Coventry's social clubs circuit. They had success with their single 'My Girl/Dark Eyes', released on the Decca label in 1976 and toured abroad.

Local jazz rock band Khayyam played at the Earlsdon Cottage on Thursdays around 1973/74. They went on to a residency at the famed Ronnie Scott's in London and later went on a European tour with John 'Bo' Bargent as road manager.

Punk band the Wild Boys achieved local fame and popularity in Coventry in the late '70s and were soon doing gigs all over the UK, including a London tour. Most of their notable

TONIGHT, MONDAY, 10th,
at
THE GOLDEN CROSS:
KHAYYAM
PLUS DISCO,
Admission: 20p.

songs were written by original founder member Roddy Byers, including 'We're only Monsters', a hit in 1980.

What did that growing fame feel like? Rob Lapworth, former bass player, tells us.

Wild Boy Rob Lapworth: surprised to hear himself on the radio! Photo: Rob Lapworth

"I was 18 and my day job was at the ICA Photography studio on the Stoney Stanton Road. One day I got home from work and mum was listening to the radio - she loved music - while making dinner for me and my brothers. Emperor Roscoe's Round Table was on. He'd just finished reviewing a Bob Dylan record and put on some new record. I wasn't taking much notice, I was hungry and the waft of food was more important! Then I thought I know this song... it was me and my band, The Wild Boys! We were on primetime national radio being discussed by famous musicians. Jimmy Pursey said "give me the Wild Boys over Bob Dylan any day". It was so strange listening to myself on the radio!"

DJ John 'Bo' Bargent, Khayyam's European tour road manager

They had a large following and caught the attention of record companies with some success. But as 2-Tone came to the fore in the late '70s, some bands, whilst still popular, were perhaps considered to be already out of date. The Wild Boys continued into the early '80s before splitting up.

The sassy Swinging Cats formed at the end decade. Labelled a 2-Tone band, they had a touch of the B-52's about them. The talented John Shipley was a member who later went on to join Special AKA.

Valerie Haudiquet stood in for vocalist Jane Bailey for a short, but memorable time. They performed 'Away and Never on a Sunday' on the 'Look, Hear!' programme in 1979. Val was the band's vocalist in the Battle of the Bands, which they won. She said: "We weren't sure we could be in the final with a substitute member of the band" - but it obviously worked.

Rex Brough remembers Swinging Cats winning this competition at the Lanch because "they were so much better than anyone else".

Their single 'Away/Mantovani' was highly praised but sank without trace despite the first 20,000 copies being sold at the giveaway price of 50p. Clearly a miss that should have been a hit.

Val Haudiquet toured with Swinging Cats and Selecter

KEEPING UP WITH THE LATEST TRENDS

CHAPTER 11

Marks and Spencer in the Precinct

Black and White Star top- on trend in the 70s!

The '70s might be the derided by some as the decade that fashion forgot but for anyone down in the trenches - well it was youth subculture heaven. Punks, skinheads, mods, rockers, rudeboys, rudegirls, straights - the never ending lists of tribes had an insatiable appetite for clothing and hairstyles that did their utmost to push the boundaries of acceptability.

> Mark Rewhorn: **"Definitely C&A for me. You could buy a suit with an extra pair of contrasting trousers for casual wear."**

We saw mini and maxi skirts, bin liners and safety pins, loons, flares and hotpants, rock chick chic and man-about town, Bowie clones, 2-Tone black and white and vertigo-inducing platforms. A bit of retail therapy, or simply shopping as we called it then, was fun and most of us went to great lengths to get the look just right.

Sensible types went for smart casual but some fashionistas perhaps should have looked in the mirror first - or maybe not, it was the 1970s anyway. "You're not going out looking like that are you?" - was the familiar (and mostly ignored!) question asked by concerned mothers the length and breadth of Coventry.

Coventry's shops did their best to cater for all tastes - or there was always the mail order ads in the back of music papers like 'Sounds' and the 'NME' if you wanted something more specialist.

The city had the usual chains in the Precinct with British Home Stores and Marks and Spencer facing each other off. Many a young man bought their gear at Burton's Menswear in Broadgate. Meryl Barrett and her friends often looked at the clothes in Chelsea Girl, fantasizing about what they would buy if they could afford it.

The old and the new: Coventry's shopping Precinct

Woolies may not have been fashionable but had all sorts of goodies on offer. Many young Dirty Stop Outs served their time as Saturday assistants to earn money for records and clothes. It was also the place to go for the forerunner of the selfie: the coin-operated photo booth.

Young people hung around to get their strip of four photos to prove they had been in town looking cool (cool in this case regularly consisted of sticking up two fingers at the camera or cramming as many people as possible in the booth). Few of the shots would ever have ever passed as passport photos it had to be said.

> Meryl Barrett: **"Skinner jeans sometimes with tartan turn-ups, Ben Sherman shirts, seggs in your shoes, and Crombie coats. There was a phase of black smock type coats with tartan bibs too!"**

More up-market was Coventry's first department store, the very fine Owen Owen's, which overlooked Broadgate. Founded in 1937, it was bombed during the war, rebuilt and reopened in October 1954. It was ahead of its time in having a woman as its manager, Miss Pinnock, who oversaw 1000 staff working in its 100 departments.

Staff were knowledgeable about the products, well trained and smartly attired. Owens stocked everything

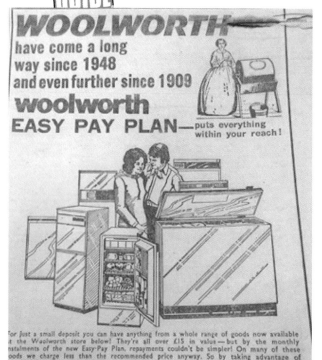

WOOLWORTH have come a long way since 1948 and even further since 1909

woolworth
EASY PAY PLAN—puts everything within your reach!

For just a small deposit you can have anything from a whole range of goods now available at the Woolworth store below! They're all over £15 in value—but by the monthly instalments of the new Easy-Pay Plan, repayments couldn't be simpler! On many of these goods we charge less than the recommended price anyway. So by taking advantage of the Easy-Pay Plan, you increase your buying power further still! What's more, having arranged credit at the Woolworth store below, you can make your repayments at any Woolworth store. The Easy-Pay Plan covers everything illustrated—and lots more besides! Come in and find out full details—and choose any item—now.

It's well worth shopping at

⊕ WOOLWORTH
EASY PAY PLAN AT
THE PRECINCT, COVENTRY.
60/62 THE P...

Ruth and mum in Woolies photo booth

from cleaning utensils to lingerie and perfume. 12 assistants worked on ladies stockings alone! What they didn't know about pantyhose isn't worth knowing. Owen's sales were legendary and crowds queued in eager anticipation.

Austin Reeds was a rather upmarket menswear store at the far end of Hertford Place. Richard Hill "was a young bloke in the 1970s" and took up a job as trainee manager. "My tenure at Reeds didn't last long. The prospect of missing more of Coventry City's home games was simply unbearable. I had also set my sights on becoming a hippy – long hair, tie-dye t-shirts, loons and the rest."

For the Love of Loons

Among Coventry's great independent shops was much loved I AM in Hales Street.

Trev Teasdel dealt with I AM's advertising in Coventry's Hobo magazine. "In August, 1973, they gave me a free pair of bright red, flared loons on condition I told people where I got them. I wasn't too enamoured by the colour at first but the price was right! They even sent me a Christmas card - that was bright red too!"

Trev Teasdel's I AM Christmas card

The lads out together!

Valerie Haudiquet: **"I AM! Great shop! Ahead of its time as shops go. Posters and jewellery downstairs if I remember right. Oh, the glorious smell of joss sticks!"**

Mark Rewhorn was quite partial to I AM's loons whilst local musician John Hewitt didn't need to buy any as his mum made him a pair.

"Mum was good at altering outfits and turned some trousers into a pair of brown and black loons."

There was a tartan craze earlier in the decade - all kicked off by the popular teenybopper Edinburgh group, the Bay City Rollers. Young girls screamed and fainted at the height of their fame as Rollermania took hold.

John D'Arcy's favourite brand- Dickens shirt

John D'Arcy bought Dickens branded shirts in the '70s which all had different small patterns and logos on them, such as Laurel and Hardy's funny faces.

The Dizzy Heights of Fashion

Dolcis had an impressive hold over the nation's youth as it did its best to corner the market with the advent of platforms - the footwear enigma first let loose on the world in 1971. Many would argue they should have come with a health and safety warnings considering the height of some of them. Dolcis were soon selling them in the hundreds. Brenda Cherrington didn't need telling twice. "Three inch heels and a bar across the front. I went to the Locarno dance night and nearly broke my neck a few times!" Brenda wasn't the only one who took this high-level fashion risk.

In 1974 Sue Lowe had her eye on pair in Dolcis. "They were bright blue. I saved up for them but as I only earned about a quid a week working in Mr Cooper's newsagents after school it took a while. I still remember

Sue Lowe: **"I remember walking from the bus stop by the station, to the Rocket pub - only a matter of a few yards. It took me ages. But I absolutely loved those platform shoes."**

how elated I felt when I finally had enough to buy them. I could hardly walk but that didn't matter one bit!"

Linda Kendall also had to save up to get herself a pair from the chic Saxone shoe shop: "I'd bought them myself out of my pay from my Saturday job stacking shelves at the VG shop on the Daventry Road."

Valerie Haudiquet bought "the most uncomfortable platforms" from Clogs shoe shop by Pool Meadow bus station. 'I stupidly danced in them all night at Mr George's. I fell down twice in the blessed things."

The place for platforms! Dolcis shoe shop

Not wishing to be left behind, the lads also went platform-shoe crazy to emulate the look of many male pop stars. Nick Edgington said: "My school -all boys - banned football in the playground while wearing platforms, especially slip-ons. Lots of them flying off feet after taking a shot - one went through a window!"

Coventry Dirty Stop Out John Starkey liked the styles of the '70s so much, he was inspired to write a poem about them:

Sharp as a pin in bottle green flares,
Peacock boy, everyone stares.
Platform heels, four inch high,
Walking tall, I can touch the sky.

With my bottle green flares,
And my platform shoes,
I can dance all night,
To the soul and blues.
(Extract from Peacock Boy)

Mrs Pearson's bargain shop
Photo: Rob Lapworth

The market

But platforms had stiff competition:- Doc Martens had been around for a long time and were adopted by several youth cultures. Dixons discount shoe shop behind the Port O'Call pub in Earlsdon was a great place to get a pair according to Nick and John D'Arcy. John loved his Oxblood red Docs which lasted "absolutely ages".

Coventry Market, 2-Tone and second-hand gear

Many great outfits were put together from stalls in Coventry Market which is now a listed building. In amongst the fruit and veg were clothes and accessories at reasonable prices. Mark Rewhorn went to the popular Deakins stall which sold most brands and sizes of jeans.

> Pete Chambers: **"2-Tone was a bit of borrowing from this and that, as long as it was in black and white! From pork pie hats, tonic, mohair suits and more."**

The distinctive 2-Tone style had made a big impact on Pete Chambers. He remembers "from schools to youth clubs, in the shops and bars and nightclubs, the black and white brigade was growing!"

It was to the market that Pete Chambers headed, pounds notes at the ready, to buy that "prized Harrington jacket", and there better be a plaid lining or else. Many rude boys had their favourite band printed on the back in HUGE letters.'

Pete's all-important mirror test was:
- Oxblood Doc's shining for England - check!
- Red braces heaving your carefully ironed white stay-press trousers a good seven inches above your instep - check!
- Blue and red Brutus button-down shirt- check!
- Porkpie hat rakish as you like - check!'

Some style-seekers raided the second-hand shops on Far Gosford Street to find what they needed, as did bargain hunter Nick Edgington. "Most of us bought three-button narrow lapel suits second hand but one friend had a tonic suit made for him."

In the late '70s Rob Lapworth and his Wild Boys bandmates favoured a shop ran by Mrs Pearson, sometimes called 'Ma'. "We, all the punks, used to go there to buy brothel creepers and winkle pickers. The shop was opposite the Coventry and Warwickshire hospital." He recalls that The Specials went there for their clothes as well.

Nick Edgington confirms this: "Some of the Specials all wore second hand at first, bought in Far Gosford Street."

Rob Summerfield was a customer at Mrs Pearson's shop."I used to buy my pointy black suede shoes from there. Great shop. They were unofficial footwear supplier to our band, the Jolly Dwarfs."

Chris Long used to go to Jeans - also on Far Gosford Street. "It was a very big place with high quality clothes mainly from Germany. It was owned by my good mate Clayton Flick's family. I got some amazing clothes there, absolute classic pieces."

And if all else fails.... Make it yourself! This is exactly what Miranda Aston did when she first turned punk. In 1976, she was "still wearing denim" but that all changed after going to a Runaways concert in October 1976.

Miranda saw a group of punks, the Bromley contingent, and said she just froze. "It was like a rabbit in the headlights moment, seeing their outfits, how they looked, their confidence. I knew what I wanted to be."

She made her own outfits from then on. "I never changed my style after that. I worked at Car Bodies back then, we did upholstery for taxis. I got some black leatherette offcuts and made this black top. I bought a dog collar and with more offcuts made wristbands adding some studs I bought from the market. And stuck a safety pin in my cheek."

It wasn't only about the style for Miranda but the attitude, the challenge to the establishment. And for young women the feeling that they could be what they wanted to be, even form their own bands and not have to settle for just being the backing singers. It was about a sense of empowerment which was reflected in the style.

The search for the right style and clothes was ongoing throughout the decade. Coventry's shops and market stalls helped to meet the demands of discerning shoppers, supplying the right outfits for the ever-changing trends.

Mrs ('Ma') Pearson outside her shop Photo: Rob Lapworth

**Perfect Punk style as made
and worn by Miranda Aston**

And what was going on with hair?

Long hair was in vogue for much of the first half of the decade but punk soon rode roughshod through that. The movement's trend for dying hair very bright colours - even having spots and stripes put in - was enough to turn some parents hair grey. Over in Earlsdon Street, Michael Morris was busy doing 'tints' at his Mainly for Men salon. Rixom's hair salon also did this hard to ignore hair tinting.

The result was young Dirty Stop Outs flaunting their 'blue mood', 'pink charisma' or 'bloodthirsty red!'

LETTING COLOUR GO TO YOUR HEAD . . .

IT'S ENOUGH to turn Dad's hair grey. Not only have we got long-haired youths, but now we've got them with coloured hair.

And it seems to have gone to the head of quite a few youngsters, who have spent up to a fiver for the privilege of having colour in spots, streaks and stripes, and even over the whole thatch.

For the more modest extrovert there are streaks of colour, at around £3 for one tint. They can range from a gentle blond to a bloodthirsty red.

Chris Moor, a 25-year-old worker with a building company, knows what it's like to walk the streets with coloured hair, as he now wears a coloured tint called "blue mood."

Tinted green

"At first you feel self-conscious, wondering whether people think you are effeminate. But after a while you get used to it, and it's nice to have something that's a bit different," he says.

Steve Holt, a 24-year-old car salesman, has his hair tinted with "green envy," and describes the style as just an extension of modern clothing.

Michael Morris, owner of the Mainly for Men salon in Earlsdon Street, Coventry, was the man who did their hair, and he explained the basic technique.

"You use a peroxide to expand the hair, so there

Story: MARTIN KING
Picture: DERRICK WARREN

is a hollow down the middle. Then you put on the colouring, which fills the hollow and gives the colouring," he says.

The couple pictured above are Christine Street and Steve Connolly, who are both 17-year-old apprentices at Michael Rixom's hair salons.

Steve Connolly said that he liked his hair dyed emerald green because he was an extrovert and enjoyed being looked at.

Temporary

Christine Street has "peacock blue" hair at the back and "pink charisma" at the front, and it will probably last anything between one and three months.

The colour has to grow out, and only the new hair is the natural colour, although temporary tints can suffice for a special evening out.

You may scoff and say: "That will NEVER catch on!" But remember that is what people said about long hair when the Beatles came on the scene.

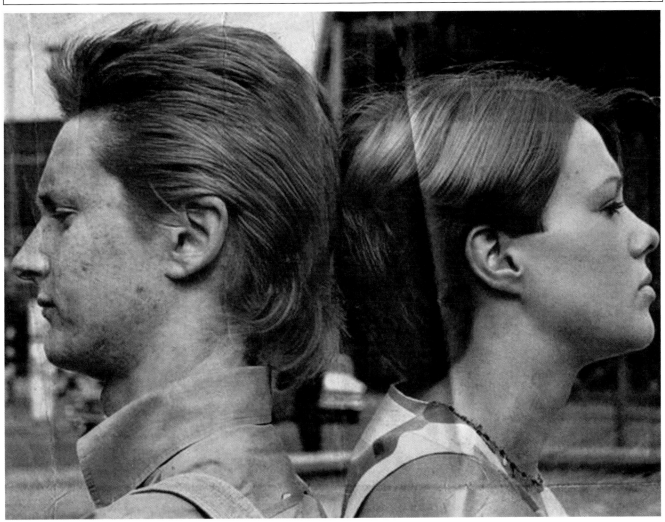

Colourful Hair!

The Precinct

You must be having a laugh?!

The legendary C. R. Garlands in Lower Ford Street stocked everything from snakes to spook the in-laws, funny masks, magic tricks and more.

It was a very special place for Luke Garland.

"The shop was opened by my granddad and gran, Ron and Eileen Garland, in the late 1960s. It only sold second hand clothes at first but later added tricks and jokes. The front half of the shop had a vast array of jokes such as masks, googly eyes and x-ray glasses, magic/sugar snake tricks, bang snaps, novelty noses and ears, magic tricks, hats, fancy dress and more. The back half had second hand clothes."

This combination worked well for Luke's grandparents. They ran two other shops, one on Swanswell Street, clothes only, the other on Holbrook Lane with clothes and jokes. People were always in need of something to wear and a good laugh too.

Garland's joke shop in Lower Ford Street

Ron and Eileen Garland in their shop

Two punk girls getting a look of disapproval!

SEEKING OUT THE LATEST TUNES AND THE HORIZON RECORDING STUDIOS

Hanging around record shops on a Saturday afternoon was a necessary evil for Coventry's young people in the era. In the days before streaming and downloading they were the place to hear new sounds, show off your questionable fashions and generally the cool places to be seen.

Popular ones included Jill Hanson's, a long-established family firm, along with Fennell's in the Lower Precinct, another family firm. Julie Redmond's dad Derek worked for his father who owned the shop. "Dad said that Pete Waterman used to come in to buy records and have a chat".

Ron Kosys: **"Paynes in Fairfax Street was a hive of deleted treasures in the early '70s. There was a lad there who did a fantastic job in finding deleted Motown singles!"**

Department store Owens sold records on the top floor with some great bargains to be had. Ron Kosys recalls it being an "implant of the great Coventry record store Fennell's." A close school friend worked there in the early '70s and Ron still sings his praises.

"Without a doubt I, along with many others, found the staff there fantastic. My great love is Motown and Mark

at the Owens branch put on one side a copy of every single as it was released on Fridays for me. He also scoured the stock to make sure that nothing was hidden away that was needed for my collection."

It was a favourite of DJs and the ardent collector. "Copies of elusive titles could be found on the shelves at Fennell's long after they would normally be elsewhere."

There was also Paynes Music Shop and SpinaDisc. Boots even sold records in the basement of their old shop for a while.

Colin Horton remembers Pete Waterman's first record shop, the Soul Hole, between the Shambles arcade and Smithfield pub. "He then moved to a shop near the Climax Pub in the Arcade before Virgin took that over."

For Sue Lowe, it seemed "so very grown up" to venture into the Virgin shop, opened in 1973 in the City Arcade.

This small shop, part of the early Richard Branson empire, added another level to the record buying experience.

Record bought at Hanson's record shop

And when Pete Waterman moved his Soul Hole upstairs in 1974, it soon became a must-go-to venue for Dirty Stop Outs keen to keep up with music trends and to buy the latest discs. Or to just hang out, waiting for your turn to listen to the latest sounds on the headphones or chat with staff. Soul Hole was a good place to find rare soul imports.

Raymond Gower: **"Great days buying punk records from the Virgin shop. I can remember John Bradbury (Specials) and Stu Napper (Riot Act) working behind the counter there too. Halcyon days indeed."**

Mike O'Hare and Malc who ran the Virgin shop "lived and breathed the music, enthused and argued over it around serving the customers".

Later on customers might bump into the likes of John Bradbury of the Specials, John Coles of Silk Disco and other local faces.

Virgin was the "first choice" for the Rhythm Doctor and he ended up working part-time there. Later he had his own department on the 2nd floor of Jill Hanson's, selling Jamaican reggae, jazz funk and post punk.

In the late '70s John Willcox, aka DJ Johnny Cocaine, worked at the Electronic Services shop in the Arcade, very near to the Virgin shop. He spent many lunch times there.

"At some point I started helping out during my lunch hours and then going back to the electronics shop." John later got a job working at HMV and his passion for music led to a different career path and moving to the USA.

Another lunchtime browser was local music writer Pete Clemons who worked at the GEC nearby in Spon Street. "Every lunchtime would find me wandering through the city centre past the clubs and record shops, searching out the latest releases and finding out who was on where."

Never one to miss out on a bargain, Nick Edgington remembers Virgin and Jill Hanson as cool places but Woolies being cheaper! "As soon as a single left the top 20, Woolies put it in a bargain bin at half-price. I spent a lot of time rummaging in that bin!" For soul

The Virgin shop in the Arcade

Above: **Hits and Misses record shop** Photo: Rob Lapworth
Inset: **Hits Misses and Vintage advertisement designed by Pete Willow**

The Sweet on Parlophone

and Motown fan, Liz Smith, Woolworths was also "my go-to place for records" though she remembers Pete Waterman upstairs in Virgin back in the day.

Trev Teasdel was inspired to mention Woolies records section in one of his poems:

Think I'll bruise 'round Woolworth's,
Whilst the sun is hiding.
Browse through the record sleeves,
New releases I am seeking.
(From Search the Crowd)

He wrote this in a café after walking around the Precinct and being sold some lucky heather. "I had in mind the atmosphere of 'Summer in the City' by the

The shopping Arcade

Lovin' Spoonful! It was playing in Jill Hanson's I think when I was jotting down lines."

People didn't always have to splash the cash to listen to their favourite records as Robin Moorcroft reminds us. "The Coventry Record Library had a brilliant blues, R 'n' B, jazz and even an esoteric folk section."

And there was also the second-hand option!

The Rhythm Doctor speaks of "two second hand shops that stick in my mind where I got some incredibly special records which I still own and play to this day." These shops were Hits Misses and Vintage records in Far Gosford Street and In and Out Sounds, Lower Ford Street.

Hits Misses and Vintage was one of Cheryl Swann's favourites as she lived local. Pete Willow recalls the "happy times browsing through the vinyl" there. "They advertised in Folks Magazine and I came up with the artwork of a dog growling at a gramophone horn which they adopted and reproduced on their front window."

Rob Lapworth also enjoyed dropping into Hits and Misses. "That sure was a great shop. Spent many hours looking for bargains and chatting there."

Ian Green: **"Hits and Misses was probably my fave record shop as with my meagre budget I could afford to buy from there. I remember the word going round my friends in 1976 there was a shop where the average price for LPs was £1.50 - at the time new albums were about £3.50".**

The Rhythm Doctor still loves vinyl!

Horizon studio Courtesy of Mark Rider

Pete Chambers: **"Horizon Studios was 2-Tone central - so many classic 2-Tone tracks were recorded there. It was a really important studio for Coventry."**

Horizon Studios

With so much going on music-wise in Coventry, it's not surprising that the city had its own recording studios. Horizon. It opened in the '70s and became an important place for local musicians wanting to record their work.

Pete Chambers: **"What bands always remembered was having to lug heavy amplifiers up the stairs."**

Local musician Ray Barrie visited before it opened and met up with the owner Barry Thomas. "He told me of his ambition to open a recording studio that Coventry would be proud of. I knew what he meant when I noticed an art student from the Lanch carefully painting part of a mural in the reception area showing the town centre and spires."

Ray Barrie soon decided to record at Horizon. "It was starting to earn a good reputation in the local musician's community. Also, the studio quoted very favourable rates!"

The studios were conveniently located near to the train station but inconveniently at the top of a multi-storey, ex-railway building with no lift! Ray recalls "laboriously lugging heavy amplification and other equipment up a steep stairway to the studios." Not easy but they did it!

Tape of recording made at Horizon Studios Photo: Ray Barrie

"The engineers and producers at Horizon also helped in our creative process with a relaxed atmosphere which made recording there so much fun", added Ray.

Ray gathered together some musician friends one time and used Horizon to record two demo songs that he had written: 'American Girl' and 'Times of Our Lives'.

Many bands used the studios including the 2-Tone artists such as the Specials, Selecter and Bad Manners. Ray reminds us that many other local artists and bands also recorded there. "They represented Coventry's rich and diverse music scene in a variety of genres, from folk and blues to punk and new wave." He and his band Reflex had a recording contract there.

They were all helped by local Grammy award-winning record producer Roger Lomas who soon got Horizon Studios noticed across the country.

Horizon Studio is now commemorated by a plaque on the wall of Coventry's train station.

Ray Barrie and Reflex band, Horizon studio with the Coventry mural in the background

CHAPTER 13

HAMMER HORRORS, 'FOREIGN' FILMS AND SUNDAY AFTERNOON DATES

No shopping on Sundays. Shops closed and pubs only open for a few hours. But cinemas were open and offered an alternative to slumping in front of the telly sleeping off the Sunday roast. Out of town multiplexes weren't yet the thing with plenty of city centre cinemas, many within walking distance of Pool Meadow Bus Station.

Most dated back to the 'golden' pre-war era when there was no telly or bingo halls to compete with. The ABC in Hertford Street used to be the Empire, the Odeon in Jordon Well formerly the Gaumont. In Tile Hill, the Godiva was previously the Standard, after the nearby motor works.

Sue Lowe and her husband, who met at a rock disco in the Bear pub, had their first date at the cinema in October 1974. They saw a film set to become a classic, Papillon, starring Steve McQueen and Dustin Hoffman. Later they saw several Hammer House of Horror films, a Sunday afternoon speciality at Theatre One. "We'd watch these films before going to the station where I saw Brian off on his train back to Yorkshire."

Whether it was kissing in the back row, watching the latest Western, horror or 'foreign' flick, cinemas were a big part of life way back then.

> Sue Lowe: **"I clearly remember 'To the Devil a Daughter' and 'The Devil Rides Out' around 1974/5, along with various Count Dracula movies, and 'The Mummy'."**

Theatre One in Ford Street, next to the Elastic Inn, was formerly the Alexandra and there was the Paris in Far Gosford Street. These two cinemas screened 'foreign' films and had 'strictly adults' cinema clubs.

Over at the Paris, there were some risqué films with 'Women in Love' (some nudity) and a 'foreign' film- 'A Man, a Woman',' more naked bodies. Mrs Whitehouse would not have been amused. The Godiva Cinema was offering something more mainstream, 'The Battle of the Bulge'.

Teenager Linda Kendall and her friend Sheila were eager to find out exactly what the 'X' was in 'X rated' films. "When a double-bill of 'Shaft' and 'Shaft's Big

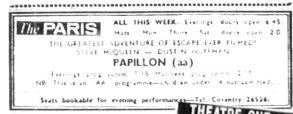

Score' was showing at the Odeon, we decided to go and see it. We didn't know much about the films other than that they were 'X rated' so we assumed there would be lots of sex."

They had resisted the allure of 'Sexy Suzy Sins Again' at Theatre One thinking that "there might be a little bit too much sex, and probably be dirty old men in the audience".

But how did they pass as 18 to get in? "As we were only 14, we knew a bit of work might be needed, so we bought some blue eyeshadow and put that on and wore our hotpants and platform shoes. We thought we'd look trendy as well as tall enough to be 18. We must have looked ridiculous tottering along to the matinee."

The films didn't further their sex education much at all. "The only sex was seeing the woman's long nails scratching Shaft's back, the rest was all fuzzy and obscured, leaving everything to our imagination, if only we'd known anything about what we were supposed to be imagining!"

Robin Moorcroft remembers Theatre One putting on a series of art house films including 'A Clockwork Orange', released in early 1972. Stanley Kubrick's film, based on the novel by Anthony Burgess, was controversial for the violence carried out by the young gang members led by Alex.

After a number of 'copy-cat' crimes, Kubrick himself decided to withdraw the film from general release. 'Clockwork Orange' then became something of an cult film and the self-imposed ban remained in place till after Kubrick's death in 1999.

Robin also recalls the premiere of 'Danish Blue', which certainly wasn't about cheese. "This drew all the critics from London, as it was billed as a new type of adult film, but it turned out to be just soft-core porn".

Late December 1977 saw the release of 'Star Wars' which was an immediate hit.

Nick Edgington used to go to the ABC Minors as a teenager. "My fondest memory is of going to see 'Quadrophenia' there in 1979 with my friends, all wearing our 2-Tone rude boy suits. As we left, and walked down the stairs, people queuing to get in saw us and started calling us "mods." So we started chanting, "we are the Mods", just to scare them!

Mods they were not but these young rude boys must have been an impressive sight in Coventry's new style.

1978 was a bumper year for films with Christopher Reeve flying across the screens as 'Superman' and John Travolta strutting his stuff in that white suit in 'Saturday Night Fever'. He was soon back dancing with Olivia Newton in 'Grease'.

These box-office successes influenced music and fashions across Coventry's night clubs - like it did across the whole country - and dancing to the disco beat was huge.

ANTHONY BURGESS

A CLOCKWORK ORANGE

Clockwork Orange, the book

Sue and Brian Lowe who had many Sunday afternoon dates at the flicks!

Celebrating HOBO! Coventry music and arts magazine

2023 marks 50 years since local music magazine project Hobo was co-founded by Trev Teasdel and DJ John 'Bo' Bargent. It was intended to 'liven up and promote Coventry music' and it certainly did just that!

It listed gigs and venues, had reviews, poems, pics and adverts for record and clothes shops. It was a not-for-profit venture and ahead of its time in many ways.

The first issue was printed at radical bookshop the Left Centre. They had an offset litho donated by historian E.P. Thompson, a lecturer at Warwick University.

Distributed free at first, it later sold for a few pence to help cover costs.

Craig Ward of The Sunshine Music agency in Gulson Road kindly let Hobo use the typewriters in their offices. This was "great" according to

Trev Teasdel as local musicians were popping in all the time and would be mentioned in Hobo.

DJ Pete Waterman - who ran Soul Hole records - used Hobo for advertising and created the Soul Hole Chart for them. Mike and Malc at the Virgin record shop also supported it through advertising and sold copies there plus wrote reviews and articles for the mag.

When John Bargent left to roadie with local band Khayyam it was a struggle to keep it going. Trev's girlfriend printed one issue at work and some further editions were produced here and there. The magazine managed to keep going till 1975.

But Hobo was more than a magazine. It was an innovative project in doing outreach

work through music with young people, especially from disadvantaged backgrounds.

This included creating a space to help new bands and artists get started and for creative activities. Hobo received backing from the City Centre Project - a youth project created by Coventry Voluntary Service Council.

By 1974 Trev and youth worker Bob Rhodes had started the highly creative Hobo Workshop gigs. To publicise their work, they organised a concert one September Saturday morning in the shopping Precinct.

Several local bands and folk performers were lined up to play and all necessary permissions gained. But the concert was soon shut down by the police for being 'too noisy!'

Local music writer Pete Clemons later wrote of how Trev and Bob's remonstrations got them nowhere: nothing could keep the music going.

An article soon appeared in the Coventry Evening Telegraph and a week-long protest in the press then ensued. Band members claimed they were persecuted for trying to do something worthwhile. Many people complained about the shoddy treatment of the Hobo team and the musicians.

But all publicity is good publicity as they say. Trev said: "We organised the concert to draw attention to the work we were doing and the police closing the event down resulted in seven days of free press coverage, much more than we could otherwise have hoped for!"

At Hobo's Holyhead Youth Centre base there was much going on. The early sounds of reggae were heard in the basement thanks to Charley Anderson, Desmond Brown and Neol Davies.

The Workshops played an important role in the development of local talent, including 2-Tone musicians. They gave first gigs to many bands such as Analog who later formed the Reluctant Stereotypes.

The Workshop moved to the Golden Cross in 1975 where Neol Davies organised a jam session with some of Coventry's top names.

Thanks to Trev's efforts, Hobo is now a detailed online archive and great resource that captures the history of Coventry's lively music scene.

Why not take a look when you have the chance?

https://coventrymusicarchives.blogspot.com

The Coventry Arts Umbrella Club and Arts Lab

The much-loved Arts Umbrella Club officially opened in 1955 in Little Park Street with popular radio comedians The Goons - Spike Milligan, Harry Secombe and Peter Sellers, in attendance.

It quickly became an important venue and a driving force for music, art, folk, poetry and literature in Coventry and continued into the 1970s.

Various members of The Midland Theatre Company along with the City Architects department were co-founders with support provided by West Midlands Arts.

The club aimed to promote all types of musical and artistic ventures and projects.

Many well-known musical and literary figures were associated with it over its lifetime, from Coventry poet laureate Philip Larkin to 2-Tone musicians. Several generations benefited from the work done by the Umbrella and the legacy it left.

Terence Watson, a poet and an English and Art teacher at Coventry's King Henry VIII school described the Umbrella as:

"Like no other organisation, it provided opportunities for development of latent abilities in creatively minded people."

There were no paid officers with people able to get involved and run events on a voluntary basis. Some long-term collaborations were formed and many friendships forged.

Al Docker and Trev Teasdel were first drawn to the Umbrella by a weekend festival of underground arts called The Transcendental Cauldron. It had local bands, underground films, artworks and poetry.

In the early 1970s, it moved away from just traditional forms of art to embrace the new emerging culture.

Al and Trev were very proactive at organising events. "We had bands on from 10pm to 2am and some that played the bigger venues played for us - Fresh Maggots, Gentle, Asgard, April, Ra Ho Tep."

Robin Moorcroft was a regular when it was based at Queen Victoria Road. "I'd go there with friends. There were bands, poetry readings, films and places to hang out. It was not just about music but also literature, poetry and art."

Many of those involved gained useful experience and skills and went on to organise events, not just in Coventry, but wherever they ended up living or studying.

In that sense, the Umbrella Club was another 'made in Coventry, sent to the world' phenomenon.

In 1972, the Umbrella had to move again due to redevelopment. When it reopened at the Charterhouse in 1974 the gigs had to stop as this protected, historic building might have been damaged. Other events continued there for some years.

Although the Umbrella lacked a formal base after the '70s, some members continued to meet, read and write poetry together in each other's home for many years.

Tea and Symphony programme but someone spelt Neol Davis's name wrong!

Pete Chambers

Pete could be described as typical Coventry kid but his love of music, especially of the 2-Tone variety, meant his life was far from typical He made a career out of his passion for music. Along with his wife Julie, he continues to play a key role in all things 2-Tone /Coventry music related.

Among Pete's many accolades as music writer, historian, museum curator and campaigner you'll find an Honorary Doctorate of Arts - from Coventry University of course. Plus 'Points of Light' Awardee music columnist and a BEM. Very impressive.

He's done so much, even when not so young, and not just for Coventry's music scene and heritage.

As a City Ambassador, he's helped put Coventry on the map many times and was instrumental in the successful bid for City of Culture status for 2021.

Pete saw many local bands play at popular venues such as the Lanch in the late '70s. It was at Mr George's in 1978 when he saw The Coventry Automatics, before they became The Specials. Actual details of the gig have "blurred with time" he says but he got his first taste of 2-Tone and was hooked.

The release of the single 'Gangsters vs The Selecter' single really triggered his sense of pride. "This was our band in my city. I recall being on holiday in Spain and skanking on the dance floor, letting everyone know that that this band come from Coventry and so do we!"

From skanking in Spain full of Coventry pride he became a music writer: how did that happen? "That was a funny one, with my musical knowledge and my English language O-Level, I just waltzed into the offices of The Coventry Weekly News and declared I was going to write a music column for them!" That was back in 1981.

Luckily for him and for his soon-to-be regular readers, they agreed. "Within weeks I was also writing a column in the Midlands music paper Brum Beat. Forty years later I'm still writing about local music, I laugh when people say, 'you know your stuff'! After four decades I really ought to have figured it out by now!"

Pete Chambers by the 2-Tone Trail plaque outside the former Holyhead Rd Youth Centre

Right: Fashion in the photo booth! A young Pete Chambers

As the Coventry Evening Telegraph's music correspondent for 12 years and regular guest presenter for BBC Coventry and Warwickshire Radio, he's always sought to highlight new talent. He also worked hard to get Coventry's once underrated popular musical heritage more attention.

Two of his key projects can be visited and enjoyed: the 2-Tone Trail and the Coventry Music Museum.

The former is a series of plaques placed at key sights that pay tribute those who made contributions to Coventry's musical and cultural heritage.

When and how did Pete get the inspirations for this? "Having written the 2-Tone Trail book that toured the pertinent sites of Ska Coventry, I figured the time was right to erect some plaques over the city."

Each one had a proper unveiling by the 2-Tone stars in the daytime with a corresponding event in the evening. It took a year to complete and was unveiled in 2009. The Trail has already been walked by countless 2-Tone fans, eager to learn more of the origins of bands and the music.

The Music Museum was "always something of a dream" for Pete and it required a lot of patience and planning to get it established. "The museum took a long while to create. Ask me about Coventry bands and I'm there, but risk assessments and fire extinguishers are entirely different things!"

The hard work paid off with November 2023 marking the 10th anniversary of the Coventry Music Museum!

A message to you Pete and Julie - thank you very much!

Pete with Coventry musician Terry Hall Photo: John Coles

Trev Teasdel

It's hard to sum up Trev Teasdel's contributions to Coventry's music and arts scene in the 1970s. He was involved in many different creative projects and was a well-known personality about town.

Trev would sometimes just hang around the Precinct taking in the sights, sounds and people and then writing about them all. "I used to go to all the relevant pubs and venues not to drink particularly but to talk with musicians and others, to organise things!" That's good old-fashioned networking.

For Trev "fun was always part of it but in the early '70s we also thought we were trying to change the world for the better, through music, art and cooperatives. What did we know!"

How did Trev find himself at the centre of so many musical and artistic events? Because he helped to make them happen in the first place and worked hard to get others involved.

At various times he has been, and still is a poet, lyricist, photographer, event organiser, editor, music archivist and creative writing tutor. His wide-ranging interests spurred Trev into organising many gigs, poetry readings, art events and general happenings across the city in a wide variety of venues.

He began writing poetry and lyrics in his teens and in 1969 was plucky enough to take his portfolio to the Beatles Apple studios in London.

He didn't manage to get past the groupies outside but later discovered Coventry's Arts Umbrella club and

Trev in action
Photo: Brian Stubley

Top: Trev in the early 70s

Above: Student Union photo

A TREV TEASDEL FOLK NIGHT

2ND "A HUMPOESIC HAPPENING"

FUN FOLK AND POETRY Rock 'N' Roll and People penturing 'CARDINAL'

WEDNESDAY ~~JUNE 21ST~~ July 12th

FROM 8 PM

THE UMBRELLA CLUB

18 QUEEN VICTORIA ROAD

COVENTRY

BRING PERCUSSION DEVICES AND instruments of all creations

Trev's Humpoesic event at the Umbrella Club

became very active in that. "It didn't have the Beatles but future 2-Toners Neol Davies and John Bradbury were involved!"

Trev along with drummer/songwriter Al Docker put on the bands at the Umbrella and co-organised an all-night Music Marathon and experimental folk and poetry sessions.

His work with the Hobo project saw Trev recognising local musical talent and helping young musicians to develop and practice their musical skill and ideas.

If you wanted to know anything about any Coventry band, Trev would know. He still does.

Trev moved to Teesside in 1980 to do a degree and stayed there: the North East's gain and Coventry's loss. But he never lost the links with his home city and continues to manage the Hobo Coventry Music Archive.

A big thank you Trev!

Musician and more- Trev Teasdel

Left: Trev performing at Merlin's Cauldron Festival 1997

Acknowledgements

A big thank you to the many Dirty Stop Outs who have enthusiastically supported my efforts to bring together stories, memories and pictures of Coventry's past nightlife, music and social scenes. What started as a small group six years ago has grown and grown. Without you all, this special edition would not have been possible! I value all you've shared plus your enduring humour, patience and friendship. The admins and members of Coventry's history and reminiscence sites are gratefully acknowledged for all they've contributed

as are John Coles, Rob Lapworth and Miranda Aston for the great photos they kindly provided. Special thanks also to Ray Barrie, John Hewitt, Richard Hil, Linda Kendall, Chris Long (the Rhythm Doctor), Lizzi Maxted, artist Carrie Reichardt, DJ John Willcox, John Starkey* and Charlotte Hendry for photos, posters, stories. To family and friends, thanks for putting up with me, yet again, talking too much about 'the book!'

John Starkey, who kindly shared some of his poetry and stories, sadly passed away in September 2023.

The author

With a lively social club right across the street from her Coventry home, Ruth Cherrington was a Dirty Stop Out from a very young age. She loved the concerts, dancing and getting up on the stage to sing. She earned top marks for having a good time long before heading to university. Her career in higher education included working abroad where she enthusiastically participated in leisure

time activities, taking note of how the local people enjoyed themselves. Returning to England, she threw herself into writing about Coventry's social history and culture with this being her fourth Coventry Dirty Stop Out's Guide. Ruth is a celebrated author and an acknowledged expert on working men's clubs and has given many interviews on TV and radio plus appeared in several documentaries.